They Told Me It Was
IMPOSSIBLE

The Manifesto of the Founder of criteo.

JB RUDELLE

ISBN: 978-1-4834-5777-2 (sc)
ISBN: 978-1-4834-5776-5 (c)

Library of Congress Control Number: 2016914520

Lulu Publishing Services rev. date: 9/7/2016

To my wife, my daughters, and my best friends, who always stood by me when times were tough—and this happened more than once

Contents

Prologue ix

1 An Unexpected Encounter 1

2 VC Survival Guide 11

3 The Art of the Pivot 25

4 It's Not about Who You Are 37

5 West Side Story 55

6 Did You Say Entrepreneur? 67

7 When Companies Will Revolutionize 73

8 How to Build the Founding Team 81

9 The Magic of Stock Options 85

10 Only the Stars Survive 93

11 The Obsession with Taxes 97

Epilogue 109

Prologue

The Lights of Nasdaq
October 30, 2013
Times Square, New York

Here I am, surrounded by a bustling crowd under an electric-blue sky. With neon signs and giant screens flashing everywhere, it feels a little intoxicating, like something out of the classic movie *Blade Runner*.

To be honest, I'm a little absentminded, tired from so many sleepless nights. And then, all of a sudden, I can't believe my eyes. On the giant screen in front of me is ... my face. Jumbo-sized! Yes, a sixty-foot-tall version of me. It's unthinkable.

And yet I'm no Brad Pitt, no Angelina Jolie. My name is Jean-Baptiste Rudelle. Sounds very French? It is, actually. People call me JB since it became clear early on that my first name was unpronounceable for most Americans. Neither my name nor my face is well known in the United States. I'm the founder of Criteo, a French start-up that is also completely unknown to the American public.

But today my little company, straight out of Paris, has been listed on the Nasdaq market. Today is the IPO, the initial public offering. And that is no small potatoes in the land of Uncle Sam. Whether I like it or not, today I'm sort of a (small) star.

This day feels like a waking dream, as if I have been split in two and am watching the events unfold as both actor and audience. I've been doing road shows for three weeks already, meeting and greeting the big money and trotting out the well-oiled story, the slick speech, tens of times—more like hundreds of times, in fact—and all this to seduce financial analysts and investors who, like Caesar at the circus, have the power to give the thumbs-up or thumbs-down on the fateful day of the IPO. I explained to them until I was blue in the face that we were about to disrupt digital advertising, that thanks to our advanced algorithms, we were able to push the right product to the right Internet user at the right time, that our business model created a lot of leverage and that the market potential was huge.

These IPO road shows are kind of crazy. You don't have a minute to yourself; you barely have time to breathe, not a moment to rest. You don't sleep two nights in the same place. You fly to a new destination every day, sometimes hitting two, even three, cities in the same day. You maintain an extremely tight schedule filled with nonstop breakfast briefings, back-to-back meetings, lunch presentations, conference calls, and group dinners. In order for us to take in so many appointments in three weeks, our banker introduced us to the supreme luxury of the powerful—the private jet. For lack of more serious drugs reserved for real rock stars, I pumped myself with Starbucks caffeine to go the distance. I don't know if musicians experience this same feeling when they go on tour, but it's both exhausting and electrifying to always be onstage. The difference is that for entrepreneurs everything hangs on the end of the tour. And of course, you don't know until the very last minute whether you did it all for nothing and you're going to beat a humiliating retreat or whether, on the contrary, things will come together in the right way and this frenetic race will finish with the ultimate accolade: the IPO.

8:00 a.m. I wear my Sunday best. For the first time since creating Criteo nine years ago, I take a suit and tie from the closet. I've worn it so rarely that it smells a bit like mothballs, but man, it's not every day you enter Nasdaq.

9:30 a.m. I take the stage. All eyes are on me. It's time to bust out a good speech embellished with a few well-chosen lines intended to go down in history. And then I realize with dread that I haven't prepared anything to say. For the past three weeks, I've been so focused on my road show that I completely forgot what came next. My mind went numb over the previous few days, during which I worked like crazy to bring on board the last few hesitant investors. Standing before me for this historic day are Nasdaq officials along with a few dozen handpicked Criteo employees and our longtime investors. There are also journalists covering the event, armed with microphones and notebooks. I think of my eight hundred other employees, who are watching us live on video screens in our offices around the world.

The audience starts to stir. They are waiting. After a few long seconds, I go for it, mumbling along. I was never a good public speaker, especially in English. But little by little, the excitement in the room starts to win me over. I warm up by explaining who we are, honoring this historic moment, and, of course, thanking the Criteo teams, without whom nothing would have been possible. I then invite onstage my two cofounders, Franck Le Ouay and Romain Niccoli, who have shared the entire adventure with me. Then the other employees in the room and our directors join us until we total fifty people onstage. It's like being in a Broadway show, and we are all a little overexcited.

Everyone stares at the giant screen. Here we are, at the crucial moment we've all been waiting for. The Criteo share price starts to form. This is when the fateful verdict will be pronounced. Will this tremendous effort pay off? Will the screen be red or green? In other words, will we make or lose money for our new shareholders, the people who chose to bet on us? During the road show, our offering was "oversubscribed," financial jargon that means demand for Criteo shares exceeded the number of shares offered. As a result, we increased our price, and following our banker advice, we ultimately offered $31 per share, $5 higher than the top of the initial price range. I now wonder, how will the market respond? Have we been too greedy? The price on the giant screen will represent our ultimate reward—or punishment.

Suddenly, the price appears in big letters: $38! A huge cheer fills the room. We are off to a good start, but it's far from over. Sometimes the price loses ground before the end of the first trading day. And that's utter disappointment. The numbers start flickering very quickly, to $39, $40, and $42, until the counter freezes at $45—a magical moment. There is nothing more concrete than this real-time price forming to show whether Wall Street believes in us or not. What stress! The clamor continues to grow in the room, reaching fever pitch. There is incredible fervor, even though it's just a share listing, not a Madonna concert or the Super Bowl.

The numbers' wild ride slows down on the screen. The frenetic blinking eases off. The price has stabilized at $42 and will continue to hover around this level for the better part of the day. $42 is very good, $11 over our offering price. But we have to hang in there until the closing bell at four thirty in the afternoon. We kill time by drinking a little champagne and giving interviews to journalists for the financial press.

At 4:20 p.m., we step back onstage for the closing ceremony. We launch orange Criteo streamers all over the place, and everyone applauds. Faces are beaming with excitement. I'm in the middle of the team, happy to feel this explosion of joy. At 4:28 p.m., Benoit Fouilland, my CFO (chief financial officer), who has joined me throughout this exhausting road show, signals to me. As usual, he is calm, but I see in his expression that something is not right. I glance at the giant screen and realize that the share price has fallen to $39. I keep applauding and smiling for the cameras, but a slight shiver runs down my spine. Only two minutes remain until the closing bell. We absolutely must hang in there so the day ends in green. I glance again, and in a matter of seconds, the share has slipped to $37, then as quickly to $36. I'm horrified, but I keep smiling and clapping like everyone else. Hurry, let the damn bell ring! These last few seconds feel endless. The market finally closes. The giant screen reveals the final price: $35. Whew, we stayed in the green. Job done.

We leave the Nasdaq building after the ceremony, motivated by our success. In Paris, Tokyo, São Paulo, and other cities throughout the world, our teams pop champagne in front of their screens. And in New York, on Times Square, we find ourselves looking around. At this moment, with astonishment, I discover my face on the jumbo screen with flashing lights. As per Nasdaq tradition, the giant screen repeats the closing ceremony outside for over an hour, causing me to do something I never do: I pull out my smartphone to immortalize this surreal image in a sort of gigantic selfie. That night, I take French leave. My bankers generously loan me their jet for one last flight, after the thirty flights I have taken over the past weeks. I head to Miami to join my wife and two daughters. I need to rest after three weeks of madness. One way of getting your feet back on the ground is trying to explain an IPO to two preteens, ages nine and eleven.

"So, girls, you see, Dad's company is divided into tons of tiny pieces that are called shares, and those shares are owned by shareholders."

"But, Dad, then it's not really *your* company?"

"Not exactly, no. It takes a lot of money for a company to run. In order to finance Criteo, we had to sell many shares to shareholders."

"What do the shareholders do with their little pieces?"

"They can buy or sell them."

"And if they sell their shares, do you lose your job?"

"Um, no, not necessarily. I mean, if they sell too many, it's not great. Actually, it's somewhat complicated, and Dad is a little tired tonight."

From now on, everyone knows what I am worth. After all the rounds of fundraising, I own about 5 percent of Criteo's capital. My financial situation surpasses what most people, including a lot of senior executives, can hope to earn in a lifetime. Of course, at this point it is mostly on paper, and my shares are subject to a tight lockup controlled by the powerful bankers. I do, however, feel that people's attitude toward me subtly changes following that fateful day. One of my friends points out that some French business magazine has included me on its list of the five hundred wealthiest French businessmen—luckily, toward the bottom of the list. After investigating, I discover that Franck, Romain, and I are included together in the same lump. It is rather funny to see us united like that. Ultimately, though, I try to disregard this financial spotlight on my personal life.

Entrepreneur: A Vocation That Wasn't in My Genes

During the month of the IPO, I often thought of my mother. She had died that summer, three months too soon to witness the event. She had cancer for several years and handled it with clear-headedness. But as is often the case with this disease, her condition deteriorated terribly during the two last months of her life. My mother was a pure intellectual. She dedicated her life to the political origins of the current French regime called the Fifth Republic. Her research was based on the observation that, as opposed to the US Constitution, which has proven remarkably resilient since independence, the French Revolution unleashed a long period of institutional instability. With the Constitution of 1958 establishing the Fifth Republic under the General de Gaulle presidency, France finally provided itself with stable institutions, institutions that allow political power to change hands between main parties without provoking a regime crisis. My mother's major focus was trying to understand why it took 169 years for France to solve this old historical conflict.

Given that she was faced with such an existential question, Criteo, Nasdaq, start-ups, and basically my whole world seemed very foreign to her. When I first started working and told my mother that I wanted to start my own company, she stared at me with concern. It really wasn't what she had hoped for me. She halfheartedly tried to dissuade me, knowing deep down that it was a lost cause. I occasionally tried to explain to her what I was doing, without getting into too many details. It's already hard enough to pitch the subtleties of digital advertising to professional investors, so the topic was really esoteric for my mother. But over the last years she understood that things were going rather well for me.

Nevertheless, my mother was used to encountering different worlds from her own. My father, an artist who specialized in *trompe-l'oeil* painting, was her polar opposite, an intuitive person who lived in his dreams of mythologized images. My father's world—painting and art—was as foreign to the Nasdaq as my mother's world. The two sacred objects in our home? Books and paintings. Everything else was secondary. With an artist for a father and an intellectual for a mother, I did not have the obvious DNA to become a business owner.

Even if we weren't rolling in money, with my father's income always fluctuating and my mother's being very modest, I still had a comfortable childhood with the right so-called social capital. I'm the youngest of four children, or rather three now. My second sister, Nicolette, drowned at sea when she was fifteen. A very gifted student with a larger-than-life personality, my sister was by far the most promising of the family. Nicolette died in a tragic accident that occurred while she was vacationing with a distant aunt in the south of Spain. Her death seemed to be the result of a series of distressingly careless and shamefully irresponsible acts. Plenty of gray areas remain over what really happened that dark evening. The only established fact is that she struggled all night long, clutching onto the hull of a sailing dinghy in distress. In the early morning, exhausted, she slipped into the water, less than one hour before her body was found. Of course, when my parents rushed to the scene of the accident the next day, no one took responsibility for anything. It was just "bad luck," as they say. What remains with me from this tragedy is a ferocious aversion to people who don't assume responsibility. My parents could have started all sorts of lawsuits, but they were wise enough to realize that it wouldn't bring their daughter back. I learned a lesson from this too. When you are stricken by some irreversible injustice, no matter how awful, it's better to move forward than to seek payback for what is lost.

This kind of tragedy certainly shakes up a family's dynamics. My devastated mother mourned for her daughter, and my father mourned for his wife. My older sister and my brother, who were eighteen and twenty, were made vulnerable right when they were becoming adults. I was only twelve at the time. Isolated from my older siblings, I learned to grow up alone, with a rather unusual image of death—not an image of old people dying, which is not joyful but is at least a normal part of life, but a shocking death, a death that struck someone down in the prime of youth and prevented her from fulfilling a destiny. Strangely enough, this kind of loss keeps those who are hit in the background. It was as if our family was surrounded by a wall of silence. I had to learn to ignore the obvious embarrassment that other people felt around our amputated family. Ever since this experience, nothing has really seemed that serious to me. Unlike most people, I feel no anxiety about dying. Death will come when it comes. I don't know if this has allowed me to dive into certain crazy projects without fear of failing. But I am definitively without the fear of being judged by others, a paralyzing fear that I have often observed in people more gifted than I.

I have to admit that I wasn't a very outgoing teenager. At first passionate about chess, I then switched to software programming. But though I begged, I never managed to convince my parents to buy a computer. In a certain way I was already a geek, someone who pursues his passions and imagination without concern for conforming to society. At the time, I did indeed have some concerns regarding social conformity. My school report cards were peppered with the word "restless," the word teachers use in France to complain about rebellious, uncontrollable students. Later on, this slight social autism became paradoxically very useful in my career as an entrepreneur. Luckily, throughout my education, my grades in mathematics were always solid, which means everything in the French school system. This allowed me to be accepted into a rather traditional but solid French engineering university. After specializing in telecommunications in my last year of college—a mistake that took me years to correct—I should have gone straight on to become an executive in a major French corporation such as Orange or Alcatel in its glory days. But I had two rather silly dreams: to create my own company and to write a book. Maybe this was my own twisted way of reproducing my parents' obsessions.

I've already mentioned that I wasn't born to be an entrepreneur. There were a few family examples of careers in large corporations, including my brother's career at IBM. But entrepreneur? For my parents, that was hard to conceive and referred to as something rather vulgar. The ultimate insult for my father was to be called a "rich pig merchant." That tells you something about his mind-set.

Still under the influence of my family, I wisely attempted to work in a large corporation. I immediately felt terrible, suffocating under orders that most of the time seemed mediocre and arbitrary. Though I tried to hang in there, I could see that it wasn't where I belonged. I was going to die of boredom in an office or more likely end up as a hermit in a shack on a lonely beach somewhere. No, being a docile manager in a three-button suit selling "man-days" in a service company clearly wasn't the life for me. As Steve Jobs said, why join the navy if you can be a pirate?

Three Companies and an IPO

When I came home at night from my salaried position, I dreamed of being an entrepreneur. I gave it a try as soon as I could. My first attempt in 1995 happened in a rush and was governed by pure amateurism. Kallback France, a call-back system for paying less for international telephone calls, was a concept I had gleaned from a smooth-talking American I'd met on a trip to the Philippines. It was a total disaster. In less than six months I burned through my entire savings and closed shop. Worse, I caused my father to lose $6,000, which was a lot of money for us at the time. I had to go back to a salaried position as a strategic consultant to build up my savings again. Three years later, like a drug addict always in danger of becoming hooked again, I became a repeat offender. My second company was called Kiwee (yeah, I know, I have a thing for the letter K), again in the phone industry but with a touch of mobile Internet since it was a business specializing in ringtones (e.g., the theme music to *Mission Impossible* or *Star Wars*). This time I did a little better. In less than four years, Kiwee had fifty employees, a turnover of $20 million, and a clean balance sheet. I was able to sell the company in the spring of 2004 for approximately one time its revenues, allowing all of my investors to do reasonably well.

Six months later, I was free. I had accomplished my first goal, creating my own company (without going bankrupt) and reselling it. And then I rather methodically moved on to writing a book with the torturous title

Why Your Lawyer Can't Pay the Babysitter, which contained my thoughts not on entrepreneurship, but on the growing inequalities within each professional category, a project that happened to thrill my intellectual mother, even though it was a complete failure in terms of readership. I did not care too much.

Once you have accomplished your goals in life, the only thing left to do is die. But given that I was thirty-five and in excellent health, it would be a long wait. What to do? I wanted to get into teaching, but after a few disappointments, I quickly realized that the school doors in France were locked shut to anyone outside of the establishment. The only choice left was my usual obsession: creating a new start-up. Kiwee had left me with an aftertaste of unfinished adventure. I also had time to think about certain mistakes I had made on this project, so I was curious to see how things would turn out if I made some adjustments. And that's how I started with Criteo (this time with a *C*, not a *K*—maybe that brought me good luck). I didn't have a magic formula, and during this new adventure, I often lost my way. We nearly went off-track several times. But we certainly showed persistence in the face of adversity. After a very rough start, the rocket finally took off in the most spectacular way. No one, especially me, could have predicted such growth.

As I write this, Criteo is now a fast-growing, profitable tech company with around two thousand employees worldwide, revenues north of a billion dollars, and a bright future. Thanks to a lot of cutting-edge technology, we are becoming a meaningful player in the digital advertising global landscape. Our algorithms, which crunch billions of data points every day, manage to capture shopping intent in real time and with stunning precision. I'm very proud to have participated in this completely unlikely, huge success story.

And in order to remain true to myself, the one thing left for me to do was, well, write another book!

Why this need? In many ways, the future belongs to the geeks. In our age where "big data" invades all sectors of business, mathematics are worth gold. We are at the start of an incredible new industrial revolution. The playing field is wide open. Let's dare to try big, hairy, audacious ideas. This means putting ourselves at risk and sometimes failing, quite often in fact. It's almost inevitable. My experience as an entrepreneur has been filled with mistakes of all kinds. But over time I learned how to make adjustments even if it wasn't a swift process. It took me fifteen years to begin to understand what ingredients make a good tech start-up. I hope that Criteo's story can help some ambitious entrepreneurs move a little faster than I did and avoid some of the mistakes I made.

I'm also writing this book to share my frustrations about the strange tendency of whining among certain entrepreneurs. Especially when I go back to Europe, I hear that income taxes are too high, that labor regulations are impossible, and so on. I'm sorry to say that if some of our start-ups fail, it's not always the government's fault.

As an entrepreneur, I still remain a citizen who questions the long-term future of a society that is growing ever more divided between winners and losers. This book certainly doesn't claim to solve every problem linked to the rising power of technology in our world. But we need at least for those who have benefited greatly from the system to get involved in the debate. For instance, people like me might need to pay more taxes in the future. What a dreadful thought! I know I'm not going to make friends saying that. But in most wealthy countries, social inequalities have gotten worse, the United States being at the forefront of this trend. It's a difficult issue, but it's an issue that is not going away anytime soon. One way or another, we'll have to address it.

An Unexpected Encounter 1

Turnips, Yes, but Organic Turnips

To think that I nearly became an expert in organic salad greens and pumpkin soup. In the most unlikely way, the Criteo adventure actually started in the back shop of a salad restaurant. Life sometimes takes unusual detours.

In early 2005, I was a little up in the air. I had sold Kiwee, my first real start-up, the year before. This experience had ended with honors and a handsome check that allowed me not only to become the credit-free owner of my home, a rather rare luxury at thirty-five, but also to enjoy the divine independence of mind that goes with financial ease. After a few months to manage the transition with American Greetings, the greeting card giant that had acquired my little start-up, I negotiated to get my freedom back. The sale of Kiwee filled me with euphoria. At this point, many entrepreneurs think that everything they touch will turn to gold, and they leap into becoming frenetic business angels by financing every start-up that comes their way. Most of the time, they lose a lot of money and end up realizing that being an investor is a real job.

I was even less clearheaded and got mixed up with my wife in an organic salad shop. We weren't organic product experts at all, or experts in the fast-food industry. *But who cares?* we thought. There was a sandwich shop next door to my old office at Kiwee. I often chatted with the owner. He was a smart guy and seemed so relaxed when he read his sports in the daily newspaper after the lunch rush. Without much thinking, I thought that his job didn't look so difficult. My wife, who was languishing in the slow-moving computer center of a large corporation—she's a geek like me—was immediately ready for adventure. So without a clue, we rushed headlong into this salad business, which proved to be much harsher than expected.

The little shop opened in May 2005 in Paris. The first day was a disaster, with only six customers. We had to toss away most of the food. It was a little grim. The second day wasn't much better. In fact, it took two long weeks of wasted quiches and soups before we felt the first stirrings of interest. Undoubtedly, this was the time necessary for word of mouth to spread about a new concept that had received no marketing. On top of this, the sad frontage still read "Butcher's Shop" because the nasty landlord had blocked any outside renovation. My wife took on the operational duties with an iron hand. I felt more like a tourist trying his hand at a small business, from making salads to running the cash register. As I served food, I learned how a business owner patiently builds clientele day after day. After a few months, there was a line outside from noon to 3:00 p.m. without a break. What a sense of pride for my wife, who had dedicated so much energy and sleepless nights!

The experience was certainly rewarding, but serving pumpkin soup, even organic pumpkin soup, wasn't my first choice as a vocation. In our store was a back shop just large enough to set up a few tables. I sat at my computer and vaguely daydreamed about a new entrepreneurial project. I knew I had to get back into the digital world. But to do what?

At the time, I often visited a place that seems prehistoric now: a video store where I rented DVDs like crazy. During this period, I must confess, I ingurgitated heaps of rubbish. Unlike what we were cooking in our salad shop, all this Hollywood crap made me feel sick to my stomach. I was repeatedly enticed by the covers but almost always was very disappointed with the contents. I cursed at myself for wasting my time, even if it wasn't worth much.

I did some thinking. To really find and watch quality movies, I needed a tool that would allow me to gather other people with similar tastes to my own. That way, we could all benefit from each other's experiences about which movies to watch. I turned over this idea in my mind. It would be easy to provide a film-ranking system via the Internet. Then with a good algorithm, it would become possible to exploit this collective intelligence to construct a personalized movie-recommendation service. The beauty of the whole approach? The more people who rated films, the more relevant the recommendations would become for everyone. So there I was tinkering with my project in the back room of the salad shop, all alone.

This was my first handicap. Slightly wiser from my previous

experience, I knew from the start that it was out of the question to go alone for my new start-up. I'd had time to think about the successes and limits of Kiwee. The project had worked okay, but I felt that we could have done much better. Being the first in France to offer personalized ringtones had been a nice marketing move, except that the market soon had been flooded with tons of clones, proposing the same commodity. Our brand, which was supposed to help us stand out from the crowd, wasn't enough to maintain our lead. The main issue was that there was no meaningful technical barrier to entry. In hindsight, our shortcoming was easy to explain. The three founders of Kiwee were all former strategy consultants, all trained in the same way. What were we missing? A real technical founder. For my new project, it was imperative that I somehow find this type of profile.

Lonely Entrepreneur Seeking Friends

How do you find cofounders when you don't have any? I just started talking about my project to anyone I knew—*a lot*. That's the first thing to do, and just forget about the don't-steal-my-great-idea paranoia. My first move was, of course, to probe my former Kiwee cofounders, even though I knew very well they weren't going to provide me with the tech skills I was looking for. This just shows how difficult it is not to follow the natural impulse to do what is familiar. I was lucky in a certain way that my former partners didn't find my concept very convincing. They had decided to explore other ideas and gently turned me down. I was disappointed. In hindsight, this failure actually put me on the right track by forcing me to fully follow my reasoning. That's often how things go.

So I was still alone. But I had no intention of sitting idly by. I had to start, even without cofounders. I knew that the more my project took shape, the easier it would be to convince someone to come on board. I had used the same approach with Kiwee: starting off alone, then employing a seduction campaign to persuade my two associates to join me. Looking hot is the key to any successful start-up. Especially at the beginning when the momentum is so fragile. Everything you do (business plan, bootstrapping, product mock-up, client tests) has only one objective: to convince the right talents to join the adventure.

The issue is that a guy alone isn't very enticing. Alone with an idea is already better. With an idea, the makings of a team, and some kind of alpha product, it starts to get more appealing. The goal? Create a sense of urgency for potential future cofounders. Convince them that if they don't come on board now, they might miss out on the chance of a lifetime. It had to be clear that I had the ticket for the *next big thing*. It would really be unfortunate to miss the train as it left the station, wouldn't it?

Of course, I had to give this train some substance so that it seemed to have life. Thanks to the sale of Kiwee, I had some money to get started. But I still had to do everything from zero. I bought a few desktop computers. Then I started to tinker with the first recommendation algorithm based on what skills I had left from my programming days, which was not much. It was very basic, but after a few days of coding, I had managed to instruct my machine that even if someone liked the first two *Terminator* movies, that didn't necessarily mean he would like the third installment of the series. I was pretty happy.

The next step consisted of recruiting two interns and a junior developer to really set things in motion. Why did I need to have some very crude software running on my desktop before I recruited a couple of interns and a young graduate? Seduction. Always seduction. Even at this stage, you want a smart intern who has good coding skills. And of course, this type of profile is very much in demand. Competing with the most prestigious companies for young talents, I had to be very persuasive to get them to join the back room of a salad shop. And convincing a young graduate from a top engineering school to trust me with his career was even harder. After countless interviews at the local Parisian café that became my headquarters for meetings, I managed to sign up my first team.

So there I was, ready to conquer the world from the back of my wife's salad shop. Even for a start-up, it was decidedly not a glamorous place to begin. I will always remember the look of the first venture capitalist who came to visit me there. The poor fellow initially thought he had the wrong address. Then he thought I was some lunatic who had eaten too much organic quinoa. Yet our little salad shop played a major part in my recruitment pitch. I was able to offer the one thing all employees value: free lunch with unlimited choice of salads, soups, and panini sandwiches. Never underestimate the seductive power of fresh tomatoes and cucumbers.

We were ready to build a decent version 1.0 of the service that would allow me to move on to the next step: introducing my project to the wide world. While you are working in isolation, it's very hard to know if you are heading in the right direction or if you are completely off-track. At some point, you need to present your project to professional investors. There is no better way to test the solidity of your big idea. Oh, you can't let yourself get discouraged by the inevitable slap in the face you will surely receive at first. Most of the time, they just don't get what you are trying to build. Never mind. That said, if after several months of pitching, not a single investor feels the need to tango with you, it's time to question yourself and consider a serious reboot of your model.

Stroke of Good Luck in the Incubator

It was September 2005, and I had a meeting with some business angels to present my project in a windowless room in a back courtyard in the Bastille neighborhood in Paris. This place was part of an incubator that housed start-ups in an open-space office with shared facilities. As I pitched my project with all the spirit that this kind of exercise required, on the other side of the table, three business angels listened to me with a slightly skeptical and weary attitude. I noticed the guy on the right constantly grinning and fidgeting with his hairy hands. I knew his condescending smile, the smile of someone who wanted me to know he was smarter than I was—and most importantly, that he was carrying the checkbook in his pocket and that if I wanted to see what color it was, I was going to have to bend to his whims. That's how it is. When you are begging for money on your seed round, it's part of the game. Being an entrepreneur sometimes also means being a diplomat. In this type of situation, I learned to put on a good face. At the end of my presentation, they dismissed me dryly: "Leave the room; we're going to discuss your case."

So there I was, pacing the incubator, my briefcase under my arm, waiting for my angels to decide whether or not I was worthy of their interest. I started chatting with some guy working on his laptop at one of the open-space tables. I quickly told him what I was doing. Pointing to a couple of desks on the left, he said,,"You should check out those two guys over there. I think they're doing something similar to you."

Really? I thought excitedly. I ran down the hallway and immediately set upon the two guys in question. It was unbelievable but true: they were working on the exact same thing I was, a movie-recommendation site.

At first, I could tell they were a little suspicious, and there was nothing more natural than that. Franck and Romain were nine years younger than I, both twenty-six at the time, and I imagine they saw me as a sly old fox ready to pounce on them and steal their great idea. On my side, I was overly excited, like a recruiter from the Elite Model Agency discovering the next Kate Moss. These two men had worked for six years at Microsoft's R&D in Redmond. They were just the perfect fit for my serial entrepreneur profile. In short, we were made to work together, and I told them so straightaway.

They were cautious. I understood this perfectly well because I had experienced these same fears when I started my first company. Like anyone, I was a little paranoid, terrified at the idea someone would steal my brilliant idea. An entrepreneur's usual first move? Hide and don't speak to anyone until the product is perfect. But this is a big mistake. Ideas on their own are worthless. Actually, the most surprising thing is that, often enough, ideas take shape simultaneously at several places around the world, as if certain things are in the air at the time. This was a perfect example. Just back from the States, Franck had built a vision very similar to mine and in a completely independent way.

Incidentally, this is why I was always a bit skeptical about the whole patent industry. It is true that in certain areas, massive long-term investments with unpredictable results are required for innovation. In this case, patents are fully justified. For example, in the pharma industry, a new drug requires years of risky testing to verify not only that it has clinical effects, but also that there aren't undesirable secondary effects. No one would leap into such expensive protocol without the guarantee of solid protection, should the drug prove to be successful. The digital world is completely different. Everything here moves so quickly that new technology becomes obsolete in a matter of years. Furthermore, most investments to test a new idea are usually rather limited. In this world, patent protection is much harder to justify. Amazon's famous 1-Click Ordering is a clever marketing idea, but is protecting it with a multiyear patent the best way to help e-commerce industry overall?

"Talent without work is a dirty old habit," said some old singer. The same goes for an idea, no matter how beautiful or innovative it is. What counts is putting this idea into execution. And that's way more difficult. The cemetery of innovations is littered with smart ideas, wonderful ghosts, and entrepreneurial dreams that never scaled. Or an innovation may be swept away by a competitor who had the same idea at the same time, but who implemented it through discipline and hard work. On top of that, most ideas require many iterations to become truly effective. Looking at many success stories, we find that the final product is very far from the initial idea. As we'll see, Criteo is a perfect illustration. What we are today is pretty remote from the original idea of helping people pick out their next movie.

Let's get back to my meeting with Franck and Romain. As I said, they were looking at me suspiciously. But I didn't care. I was determined to hook these two. I immediately pulled out the heavy artillery to charm them. I was much more fired up than in front of the business angels, who might have come out of the meeting room by now, looking to give me their verdict. I had completely forgotten about them.

The two reluctantly described their project to me. Actually, it was mostly Franck who spoke. He was the one who had started the project and had convinced Romain to join him a few months later. To show me that they were serious, he said, "We're going to raise $300,000 in a few months once the website is up."

Romain nodded slightly. I understood right away that they were very close friends.

I made a sweeping gesture and said, "$300,000? That won't get you anywhere. We have to raise $3 million from the get-go. Immediately. And as strange as it seems, you'll see that it's not necessarily more difficult."

It was a bit over the top, I admit. At the time in 2005, a seed round of $3 million for a start-up based in France that didn't really have a product to show was a stretch. Even with my past experience in fundraising, it wasn't going to be a walk in the park.

But I was persuaded that the three of us could move mountains. As investors who hated risk (a curious paradox we'll return to later), we formed a dream team. I was a serial entrepreneur who knew how to speak their language. Most of all, I had already gone through the entire life cycle of a start-up with Kiwee, from the fundraising to a trade sale that saw all the investors recoup their money, with certain venture capitalists even making a substantial return (up to five times their investment, which was very decent compared to industry standards). Meanwhile, Franck and Romain brought the credibility required to support our technology

disruption pitch. Franck is a brilliant, original mind, a very gifted concep-
tual thinker. He is behind the algorithm at the heart of Criteo's success.
This amazing engine is what has made our technology always a step ahead
of competition. Romain is very complementary to Franck, a real engineer
too, and also blessed with very solid communication and management
skills. This last ability would prove critical when our technical team went
into hyper-growth mode.

We split up that day on the possible idea of joining forces. But it was
far from done. Nothing was that simple.

We talked things over for several weeks. I tried to reassure them. My
two future partners didn't drop their guard right away. They could see
that we had very complementary personalities and backgrounds, but they
hesitated to get involved with a total stranger whom they met by chance
in a hallway. As for me, after Kiwee, I was in a different mind-set. I knew
I wanted to work with these two so much, even if I still had this little voice
in my head saying, "Are these two really serious? Are they going to walk
out on you at the first roadblock that comes along?"

A start-up is a long-term project in which success comes only—if it
comes at all—after so many difficulties and disappointments that must be
overcome. The number one quality of any founder is persistence, the ability not to get discouraged when faced with rejection. Franck and Romain
had just returned from the States. They didn't have references in Paris I
could go to. Do you know what I liked most about them? They were both
on welfare! Actually, when they returned to France, neither of them had
access to the rather generous French unemployment benefits. But rather
than taking refuge in big corporations with comfortable paychecks, they
had chosen to tighten their belts. To launch his start-up, Franck had even
moved back in with his parents. This type of unusual determination was
a good sign, not to mention that after a few rounds of discussion, I had
already started to appreciate their pragmatic and clearheaded style. The
last thing I wanted was to embark on this adventure with two people
with oversized egos. It didn't take long for me to realize that Franck and
Romain were the total opposite.

After a month of dancing around, we met in a café one night for the
critical meeting around the cap table. The discussion started off a little
tense. I restated all the value of merging the two projects. My point was
that it was way better to have a smaller part of a very big cake than 100

percent of a miniscule cookie. But they were hesitant about how to approach this. I saw the moment when everything was about to collapse. At this point, the bonds between us were very fragile, and the smallest thing could make the discussion go the wrong way.

Ultimately, we came to an agreement. I went from 100 percent to 50 percent of the capital and they split equally the remaining 50 percent. Why not one-third each or 80 percent for me and 20 percent for them? After all, I had ten more years of experience and, most of all, a successful start-up under my belt that provided me access to all the investors in the market, a key element for our project to be viable: no big fundraising, no ambitious project. On the other hand, without cutting-edge technology, I knew that it would be very difficult over the long term to protect us against competition, as I had experienced bitterly with Kiwee. So it was a subtle balance. In the end, each team brought half of the ticket to success. That's why we opted for a fifty-fifty deal. Nevertheless, it was not easy to negotiate this together. Everyone had to accept the idea of sharing. And losing control can be very stressful.

The deal was sealed. We parted ways feeling lighthearted that day, but with a slight bit of fear: what if we had just made a big mistake? Of course, there was no way we could know that we had just made the best decision of our entire professional lives.

VC Survival Guide 2

What's Wrong with Bankers?

Sharing with your cofounders is critical. Sharing with financial investors is another story. The latter is more complicated, but it's also vital. As a matter of fact, when I pitched Franck and Romain, I had based my credibility on my ability to raise funds. Now it was time to prove myself.

For a lot of entrepreneurs, financial investors seem like foxes in the henhouse, the stereotypical image of the big bad banker. There are so many small-business owners who refuse to open up their capital to investors because they are afraid of losing control. There is fear of the proverbial vulture fund that swoops in and then kicks you out at the first signs of success to steal the prize from you.

The result? Most small businesses are financed by debt. To keep their precious freedom, small-business owners seek loans from their bank. I can still see myself in my banker's office as I presented my wife's salad shop project. He greeted me with a big smile, repeating that he had a lot of experience in the food industry. And then he rolled out his conditions. All very standard, he insisted. I just had to stand surety for myself by mortgaging my home. Alternatively, the banker offered that we could also freeze the equivalent of my loan from my savings, which basically meant I was giving myself a loan. Delightful, huh? It made me realize that going into personal debt to finance projects was the daily misery of most traditional entrepreneurs.

Luckily, technology start-ups work in a different way. It is simply inconceivable to apply to start-ups the type of financial guarantees that a commercial banker demands for traditional businesses. You might find yourself in personal bankruptcy because your start-up didn't succeed? The risk is simply unreasonable. And yet it's the only option that your local banker can offer you. The poor guy can't do anything about it because he was trained to assess restaurant business plans, not tech start-ups with the ambition to change the world.

When I started Kiwee, I had a hard time just finding a bank that would allow me to open a checking account to deposit the initial capital. *Mr. Banker, I'm not asking you for a loan*, I thought. *I just want to give you my money. What the hell is your problem?*

Looking for the Next Unicorn

At this point in the story come the players who are rarely seen outside of the tech world, the venture capitalists, or VCs, a relatively young profession, especially in Europe. In France in particular, most of the VC players are heavily subsidized by the state, directly or indirectly, via various tax incentives. In the United States, VCs are drawing a steady flow of capital far superior in aggregate to Europe. Yet the return on equity for the industry on both sides of the pond is surprisingly not that great on average.

So why do investors continue to be so drawn to this sector? Because the industry's average return does not tell the full story. The top 5 percent of VC firms tend to do extremely well. That's the magic of this business. For the best, profits can be extraordinary. At Criteo, for instance, our series A investors made more than two hundred times their initial investment. What other (legal) investment offers this kind of return?

These are rare cases, but they fuel the entire system. Every investor wants to discover the next unicorn, a start-up whose company value will exceed the mythic threshold of a billion dollars. Of thousands of investments per year in the world, only a dozen will eventually reach this star status. But as during the gold rush, everyone is convinced that he or she will be the one who finds the next big thing. And money keeps swelling in the VC machine. A handful of US VCs manage to repeatedly reap impressive returns, making their partners very rich. They seem to have found the winning formula for discovering future unicorns before anyone else.

The Art of Negotiating with a VC

The way VCs act during a negotiation reveals a lot about who you are dealing with. Amateurs and second-raters fight like cats and dogs over the valuation and will quibble over every clause in the shareholder agreement. On the other hand, the best investors—the real professionals—focus on the only question that counts: does this start-up have the ingredients to become the next big thing, yes or no? These investors are very selective about their investments, but if they are convinced that a project has truly great potential, they are prepared to do anything to be a part of it. In this unique line of work, it is much more important to maximize profits than minimize losses. And to do so, above all you don't want to miss out on the key deals.

During my seed round with Kiwee in early 2000, I dealt with a friendly but somewhat amateur business angel. On the day of the closing, his right-hand man enthusiastically arrived and said to me right from the start, "JB, we're thrilled to invest in your company. But you know that your project is very risky. So you're going to have to lower your premoney valuation by 10 percent."

Premoney valuation? This refers to the company's valuation before the round of financing. It's a key number because it's basically what you are worth in the investor's eyes. In our case, we had agreed on a valuation one month before the closing. And then at the last minute, my business angel was demanding a 10 percent reduction. It felt like a bad dream.

After a few seconds, I said coldly, "If that's the case, you can tell your boss that it's over. It's all right—I have another investor who is ready to jump on board in your place."

I was bluffing. I didn't have any serious backup plan. Actually, our cash was running very low. We needed that money so badly, but at the same time, I couldn't swallow this request. If you can't trust someone's word from the start, it's a bad sign for the future.

My answer threw him. I don't think he was expecting it. Luckily, we were in the middle of the Internet bubble, and given the frenzy at the time, my threat sounded entirely credible. He quickly changed gears. "Okay then. Let's go with what we had said. But let's sign quickly so you can go back to work."

I sighed with relief—to myself, of course. Sometimes a negotiation relies on very little.

It was different for Criteo. With my serial entrepreneur background, it was easier to deal with VCs. Nevertheless, I still had to roll up my sleeves. Raising money is never an easy task. My first move was to turn to my prior investors, those who had made a good return on Kiwee. They were ready to back Criteo, my new venture. But I wasn't enthusiastic about the rather complicated financial setup they offered me. At that point, a large investment fund came into the game. The difference in style struck me immediately. The big boss, Benoist Grossman, got personally involved in the conversation straightaway. We had been talking face-to-face for half an hour. He was an intuitive person. I could see that he was hooked. I was explaining to him that I already had a term sheet from my former Kiwee investors when he interrupted me.

"JB, what's your premoney valuation?"

"Four million."

"And why haven't you signed with them yet?"

"They're offering convertible bonds. It feels unnecessarily complicated at this stage."

"I like simple terms too. Listen, we'll do it exactly as you want, and you'll have a term sheet in your in-box tomorrow night."

I was flabbergasted. Less than an hour earlier, he hadn't known me at all, and now he was ready to put $2 million on the table. I had never met someone so quick in investment decisions. The next day, Benoist kept his word. And today, I doubt he regrets it.

Stick to What You Know

In traditional small and medium-size businesses, there is often some confusion between the person who owns the capital and the person who manages it. In giving up part of his equity, the small-business owner is terrified at the idea of losing control and no longer being able to run his company the way he wants. In the tech start-up world, this fear does not make sense. VCs (at least those who understand their job) aren't there to interfere with day-to-day operations and run the company instead of the managing team. Of course, they ask for monthly business reports from the CEO. But after all, this is a healthy habit that allows a quick review of key business drivers.

At Criteo, we were confronted with this instinctive mistrust of "the big bad financier who wants to steal our company." During the first year of operations, our three founders added an ephemeral fourth musketeer. He was with us during the period when we were desperately trying to find our model and nothing seemed to be working. It was a tough time. Meanwhile, this new fourth cofounder was convinced that our investors were waiting for one thing and one thing only: to kick us out. He couldn't stop worrying about our revenues taking off and our VCs swooping in to steal the till and take our place. I ran out of ideas for trying to calm his paranoia. He was so convinced that we would be dismissed that he finally decided to take the initiative and leave on his own.

And old venture capitalist told me one day, "Look at Amazon, Microsoft, Facebook. The best start-ups are almost always carried by their founders for a very long time." He was right. You have to remember that a VC bets on a team more than on anything else. If he has to change the team, that means he has already lost his initial bet and probably a good part of his investment.

But nevertheless, many entrepreneurs seem to be endemically suspicious, devoured by an inherent fear of losing control. We had a hard time escaping this equation: dilution of our capital = loss of operational power.

At Criteo, we were so focused on maximizing growth that we managed to overcome these existential worries. I went from having 50 percent of the capital to 40 percent, then 20 percent, 10 percent, and finally, about 5 percent of the capital. But once again, it's better to have a small slice of an enormous wedding cake than the biggest piece of a miniscule cookie. Most of the time, significant capital dilution is necessary to fuel hyper-growth. However, as such, it has no bearing on your managing freedom. My ability to make decision as Criteo's operational leader was always exactly the same, no matter how much capital I controlled.

Why It's Better to Raise Too Much Than Not Enough

There is another principle related to the cake theory. My approach was always to raise *too much* money. In other words, when Criteo needed $2 million to start in 2005, I immediately raised $3 million. In 2008, we needed $5 million to expand internationally. I made sure we got $9 million.

In the spring of 2012, Benoit Fouilland, my CFO, came to me with a spreadsheet full of numbers. He seemed a little worried. We were profitable, but we had grown very fast, too fast—a rich person's problem, sure, but something that could prove to be delicate. In fact, the faster we were growing, the more money we were burning. Benoit showed me that our accounts were coming very close to the red in certain months. This situation coincided with our move to rue Blanche.

Oh, rue Blanche! Our new office space in Paris's ninth district was truly beautiful and impressive, with a futuristic lobby that gazed up at a vast atrium of steel and glass. Our rooftop with a panoramic view of all the great monuments of Paris was also amazing. Rue Blanche was a gorgeous flagship that helped convince many talents to join us. But beauty has a price. When we signed the lease, the owner naturally requested a security deposit. Our bank, which one year before our IPO still considered us to be an untrustworthy, renegade start-up, did not give us any flexibility, and we were obliged to freeze the entire deposit, $5 million. This setback suddenly made our cash position much tighter.

"Do you think we've bitten off more than we can chew?" I asked Benoit.

Previously, I had always been very reasonable about office space. With the rue Blanche site, we had decided it was time to move into a new league. But I didn't want this boost to be the straw that broke the camel's back, a self-indulgent project that would lead the company right off the cliff. Benoit assured me it was okay. There was nothing alarming about it. We just had to make one last round of financing before the IPO. According to his calculations, $20 million would be enough. But in order to think big, I decided to raise $30 million.

Of course, the more money you raise, the more diluted you become as a founder. After a few years, we had considerably less equity than if we had played it tight. But this was more than offset by two fundamental advantages. First, having (too much) cash on hand lets you sleep well at night, which is priceless. This allowed us to take more ambitious risks for Criteo. Second, it guaranteed us more independence vis-à-vis our investors—because the only time that VCs can really bother you and try to impose their own vision on the business is when you need new money. And VCs imposing their vision when they have just a superficial understanding of the business and are not in charge of day-to-day operations is the best recipe for failure. In general, experience shows that shareholders who act too much like managers create more issues than anything else.

I had learned my lesson with Kiwee. When our ringtone business started to take off, all indicators were green. I felt it was the right time to accelerate and quickly scale our marketing spend. But one of my investors started to freak out. In the middle of a board meeting, he learnedly corrected me. "That seems premature to me. You have to keep doing tests for another three months. If the numbers come back good, then we'll see."

He was a young guy starting off as a VC. In other words, he had never run a start-up himself. But that didn't prevent him from speaking with authority. He undoubtedly thought in all good conscience that he was bringing some outside wisdom to the poor entrepreneur who had his nose too close to the grindstone. Kiwee was the first time I had found myself running a real board of directors. I had this somewhat naive idea that investors were sitting there for a good reason. I was worried about doing well, a little like a stressed-out young mother who listens too closely to her entourage—her family, the nursery school teachers, and her good friends—who all supposedly know how to care for her child better than she does. I reluctantly sided with him.

Ultimately, because of this cursed quarter of useless tests, we lost a good deal of the momentum we had over our competitors. This wasn't fatal, but it made me think. Admittedly, it is always interesting to question your strategy based on outside opinions. It's healthy to ensure that the management isn't completely off the mark. Nevertheless, the entrepreneur needs to remain the final decision maker and ultimately trust his intuition, exactly as a mother will always know what her child needs better than anyone else. Of course, I am anything but omniscient. This intuition sometimes led me down dead ends. But I have to say that each time I forced myself to follow wise strategic advice from my investors against my own instincts, I ended up kicking myself.

Anticipate the Divorce So the Marriage Succeeds

Finding the right balance between the VCs and the founders is complicated but essential. This union is similar to a marriage, except that in a marriage the vast majority of people never think about their marriage contract. They take it out only when things go bad. In business, it's a different story. The approach is more rational. Most of all, everyone knows that a bad divorce can be fatal to the project. So the marriage contract—the shareholder agreement, where the rules of the game are written in black and white—must be calmly discussed point by point before the closing of the investment.

Ah, the shareholder agreement! Better to say now that it is indispensable. I also learned this the hard way with Kiwee. At the start of the project, I had met an older school alumni, a smooth talker who bragged of having enormous technical expertise in my domain. Let's call him F. He convinced me to give him 5 percent of my capital for a tiny price in exchange for his generous advice. Very quickly, F. proved to be a total jerk, and I understood that I had stupidly wasted a precious part of my equity. But that wasn't the whole story. Lulled by his fine words, I had invited F. into Kiwee's cap table without having him sign a proper shareholder agreement. This clever fellow understood that very well. So when I began the delicate fundraising process, F. started to bombard me with all kinds of absurd legal claims—the kind of harassment that makes financial investors run for their lives, especially when you are raising money for the first time.

As I was about to close my series A, my new investor said to me, "JB, we're interested in your project, but we won't sign anything as long as this troublemaker is part of your cap table."

I was verging on another cash squeeze, and I couldn't put off raising funds. I had to force F. out in the only way possible: with money. With the help of a friendly business angel, we sadly resigned ourselves to writing him a check for more than one hundred times his initial investment so that he would agree to sell his shares and leave us for good. It was that or the end of the story for Kiwee. From that moment, I double-checked all of my shareholder agreements in nearly maniacal detail.

I don't know how many hours I spent discussing this topic for Criteo. For our first shareholder agreement, which was to be the groundwork of our relationships, I found myself at the negotiating table with Marie Ekeland, who was coinvesting in our series A. Marie is one of the rare women in the inner sanctums of venture capital. She stands out from her male colleagues because of an incredible work ethic combined with a low ego, a rare quality in this business. This makes her particularly good at complex deals. Marie has no equal when it comes to finding creative and pragmatic compromises in situations where certain men stubbornly dig in their heels over so-called principles. Because of her interpersonal skills, she often found herself taking the lead over deeper pockets in delicate negotiations with the founders.

As it happens, I had to take up a rather delicate subject with her. "Marie, we have to envision the case of one of the founders leaving."

"Don't even think of it, JB! You know if you leave us, it'll be a disaster."

"Don't worry, I'm not considering it for a second. But we have to think of every possible theoretical situation in order to protect everyone."

And that led to hours of negotiation. When, how, and by how much should a cofounder be compensated if he were to leave the company? What would happen if this cofounder was forced out or if, on the contrary, he just decided to walk away one fine day? It was a little like, in writing the marriage contract, already calculating the detailed benefits of a future divorce.

I remember these discussions about shareholder agreements being rather tense from time to time. It's a sort of balance of terror; each side needs the other, and everyone is in a stare-down. It never really ends (until the IPO) because with each new round of investors, you have to go over the shareholder agreement again. Just be careful that this discussion doesn't turn into a trial of strength. Remember that you have to live together afterward, often for years with your investor. Imagine a couple on their wedding day tearing each other to pieces to have the final word. Is that the best way to start a long-term relationship?

During our 2012 series D, which was our last round before going public, Criteo was worth $600 million. This was already an incredible success. We were in the process of raising an extra $30 million to help us finance this last stage as a private company. Beyond the lofty valuation, this time we were bringing in four new investors with very different profiles, something that made the deal fairly complex. After a few months of discussion, we finally reached the final phase of the deal.

The week in which we were to finish the job came at a bad time. My wife and I had longstanding plans to go on our honeymoon to the Maldives while our daughters went to summer camp in France. But the negotiations were stuck on a financial clause that no one could agree on. Instead of enjoying the blue lagoon at my feet, I was glued to the phone in my bungalow, arguing with Dominique Vidal, a.k.a. Dom. This exceptional venture capitalist had a decisive influence on Criteo and became a friend over time (I'll get back to that later). But Dom was also my lead investor and, as such, was deeply involved in this difficult negotiation. We were going in circles. I was a little frustrated because everyone was leaning on their positions.

At one point, Dom paused and suddenly said to me, "JB, we've known each other a long time. But right now the conversation is becoming really unpleasant. How is that possible?"

I promise you, this comment shook me up. He was right. After all this time together, all the shared emotions, and in view of this incredible adventure we were building hand in hand, it would have been really stupid to have a falling-out over something so minor.

The tension suddenly dropped. In five minutes, we landed on a compromise that satisfied everyone.

The Virtues of Partial Cash-Outs

Venture capitalists often want to be hard in negotiations, sometimes too hard. Why negotiate shareholder agreements if they are then unworkable because terms are unreasonable? A good VC also knows that sometimes he needs to offer the founders some breathing room. Once the business has started to really take off, a good practice is to allow the founders to sell a little of their equity, just to have some real cash off the table. French VCs often loathe this idea. They are afraid that their promising entrepreneur will suddenly become apathetic after cashing his first check or that he will have only one idea in mind: head off to a sunny beach, kick his feet up, work on his tan, and party all night long. Experience shows, however, that in the vast majority of cases, this fantasy of the lazy opportunistic entrepreneur is not the least bit true.

Kiwee, my first start-up, was a good case study. When business started to take off, it created an unexpected dynamic. I had invested all of my savings in this adventure. With the growing success of our business, I suddenly found myself as a big shareholder in a start-up that was developing a very nice valuation. I was at the head of a tidy little sum, at least on paper. This situation was both exhilarating and paralyzing. I felt I was facing a house of cards that could collapse at any second. My lovely fortune remained virtual. Should business suddenly turn bad, which is frequently the case in digital technology, it would all go up in smoke. The consequence was that I had a hard time taking risks. We had managed to raise $7 million, but I kept a tight hold on it, spending sparingly. The practical consequence was that we systematically underinvested over the long term. We limited our international expansion to Spain and Belgium, and when we launched new products, we did it without committing enough to ensure a reasonable chance of success. In fact, after a handsome start in 2000 and very fast growth in 2001, Kiwee reached its ceiling in 2002 due to insufficient investments. When the start-up was acquired in 2004, we still had more than $6 million in the bank. Out of fear of losing it, we had never used this money. Such a waste.

For Criteo I had time to consider this issue. In 2010, the company was already profitable with very strong growth in Europe. We were about to tackle the US market, a much more difficult challenge. With $40 million in gross revenues, Criteo was valued around $100 million. At that time, this number seemed breathtakingly high to us. Statistically, very few start-ups reach this symbolic threshold. An old hand in the sector had warned me, "You'll see, when you hit a valuation of $100 million, people start to go crazy."

During preliminary discussions with Bessemer, our new series C American investors, I brought up the topic. I knew that our conquest of the US market would be very expensive and that should it fail, it could seriously jeopardize the company. But the risk was worth it. For myself, I had no doubts about going all in, as you say in poker. However, I was a little worried for Romain and Franck. They were starting families, with all the responsibilities and logistics that go with that. I sensed that they might experience the same issues I had experienced with Kiwee. They were multimillionaires, but only on paper. It was all very virtual. My new American investors quickly understood my concerns. They immediately offered a partial cash-out for the founders as part of this round of financing. In practice, this meant that a fraction of their investment would go into buying some existing equity from the founders rather than new shares only.

Interestingly, this type of partial cash-out is still quite unusual in Europe, but increasingly common in the United States. Spurred on by our new American investors, our European VCs agreed to play the game. This provided each of my cofounders with a nice check, enough to make their day-to-day life much smoother.

I remember the sale of Kiwee like it was yesterday. This first cash-out had completely changed my life too. Overnight, I had gone from being an entrepreneur whom banks refused to give a mortgage to a premium client who got the red carpet treatment.

This partial cash-out gave a new start to the Criteo founding team.

We made a mutual agreement to throw everything we had into international expansion, to invest all over, including in rather intimidating countries such as Japan, where few Western start-ups dare to venture. The Land of the Rising Sun is now one of Criteo's most spectacular successes and our second-biggest market after the United States. We also decided to work twice as hard in research and development. This wasn't an obvious choice because once the initial team perfects the product, you are particularly tempted to limit investments in this domain. After all, once the product has proven itself, why not just focus on business development? To continue investing in technology means having large fixed costs and expenses that can't be reduced easily. This is why very few companies, even in the world of tech start-ups, invest above the strict minimum, maybe because they are too tied up in short-term thinking. On the contrary, we put tremendous efforts into this area. This strategy allowed us to secure our lead over competition. This tech focus has proved to be a key success factor over the long term.

Is It Time to Sell?

Venture capitalists are looking for liquidity on their investment, often sooner rather than later. On the day of the closing of my last round for Kiwee, my new investor asked casually, "So, JB, what's your plan for the exit?"

I was a bit shocked that as soon as this investor was in, he wanted out. Now that's the mind-set of a lot of VCs, whose real nightmare is not a start-up going belly-up, but being stuck for years or even decades in a start-up. To be fair, VCs have their own liquidity commitments to their own investors, so staying too long in a venture always makes them a bit nervous. For Criteo, I must admit I was quite lucky that as soon as we got real market traction, our investors felt that there was so much potential down the road that selling too quickly would not be the best option.

Still, in early 2013, the issue came on the table in an unexpected way. I was in California when I received an e-mail out of the blue from some guy in corporate development in a giant West Coast company, asking me to meet the next day. I was not sure what this was about—probably a waste of time, I figured. Still, it was just a fifteen-minute drive from my office, so it was no big deal to accept the appointment. When I got there the next day, there were six people waiting for me on the other side of the meeting room. *Wow, man, what's going on here?* I wondered.

The guy sitting in the middle got straight to the point: "We've been watching you for quite some time. What you do is really impressive. We are here to discuss how we are going to buy you."

Okay, mister, now you've got my full attention. This was the first time someone had been serious about acquiring us. The discussion went very well that day. Actually, I really liked their vision, and after some additional back-and-forth in the following days, I had the feeling that things were getting very well on track. My investors were jumping and popping like popcorn. It was quite hard to keep everyone's head cool, especially because at this stage, we still did not have any indication of the price the company was willing to pay. But this tech behemoth had such deep pockets that anything was possible.

Then came the key meeting. It was just me and the number two of this big corporation, eye to eye. During the first ten minutes of the discussion, he talked about the US education system and why it was so much better than the systems in Europe. At first, I did not see the point. In fact, he was trying to probe how committed I was to staying on the West Coast with my family. In a way, it was a good sign that he was already thinking of post-merger integration plans. Suddenly, he changed gears and said, "So I did some thinking, and we would like to offer $1 billion for your company, all in cash. What do you think?"

It's not every day you get this type of offer. A one-billion-dollar check for my little start-up? This was a once-in-a-lifetime opportunity, and I was lucky to have it. He was looking at me, waiting for my answer. My head was spinning like crazy. Who could resist this magic-unicorn billion-dollar number? Still, there was no way I was just going to respond plainly, "Yes, that's perfect." First, any good deal involves price negotiation, and I was pretty sure that he was not showing all his cards. After all, his company had almost unlimited means, and this was pocket money for them. My investors would also expect me to put up a good fight before surrender.

Though my heart was pounding hard, I tried to answer in as detached a tone as possible. "As you might have heard, we have plans to go public later this year. We've done some rough calculations, and we estimate that in a reasonable time frame after the IPO, the company will be valued at least ... $3 billion."

Okay, man, please don't take this wrong. Nothing personal—we are just bargaining here. So now tell me, what's your real number? I thought.

After a short moment of hesitation, he switched gears and moved to another topic. I assumed that before giving me a counteroffer, he needed to run it internally. And most likely, this would involve the big boss. Even if they had done much bigger deals in the past, this amount would require the CEO's direct approval.

However, after that fateful meeting, the big corporation suddenly went dark. Two weeks later, it was obvious that the deal was gone. Had I pushed the envelope too far in my response? Hard to tell. Anyway, it was time to focus everyone back on our IPO plans. After all, that was a very exciting path too, and down this new road, the sky was the limit.

Still, for a long time, I continued wondering what really had happened behind the scenes. It was only quite recently that I learned the truth in an unexpected way. I was having coffee with one of the company's ex-employees, and by chance, this topic came up.

"In hindsight, it would have been a great deal to do. Actually, I was in the room when we made the no-go decision," he told me. "You want to know why?"

You bet I wanted to!

He continued, "It was not a question of money. The veto actually came from our tech team. They claimed they could build the same product on their own. It's funny in retrospect because I know for a fact that even today, they are still struggling to build something similar to what you guys have achieved."

The Art of the Pivot   3

Looking for the Right Model

"How many times did you pivot?"

In the start-up world, "pivot" is something of a magical word, a sign of recognition for the insiders. Among tech founders, almost everyone has pivoted, is pivoting, or will pivot at least once in his or her life. Pivoting is everywhere. There are even conferences focused solely on this concept. When, how, and why to pivot? Entrepreneurs are fascinated with this and for a good reason. Pivoting sometimes makes the difference between filing for bankruptcy and achieving success. Americans, who always have a punchy way of putting things, define pivoting as firing the plan instead of firing the CEO.

In technology, straight lines are the exception. In practice, managing a start-up is like driving a roadster on a mountain road. You had better have a strong stomach. If the original idea doesn't work, it's not necessarily because the founding team is bad. It's just that it is often very hard to see in advance which direction to take. So although you go one way initially, you drastically change the model if it becomes clear at some point that you took the wrong direction. That's pivoting. Whether to pivot is far from obvious. Implementing a sharp change in direction is anything but comfortable, especially when you have invested a lot of time and energy leading the team and the investors in one direction. But it's often a question of life or death.

In the volatile world of digital technology, even the most established players can crumble quickly. It's rather exciting to be a little guy trying to burst onto the scene and dethrone the ruling behemoths. What matters is finding the right path to disruption. Leveraging your core expertise, you have to be able to transform your model in the blink of an eye to adapt to a new situation.

Major successes today such as Apple and Facebook all proceeded by trial and error. They made mistakes and tried various models before finding the right formula. Take Google, which is probably the most powerful company in the world today. At first, cofounders Larry Page and Sergey Brin had absolutely no idea that advertising would become their cash machine. In the first years, Google tried to sell its superior search technology to big web portals such as Yahoo! But upon realizing that keywords typed into Google's search engine revealed laser-precise consumer buying intent, the team understood they could earn a lot more money by directly selling highly targeted advertising.

When success arrives, PR often rewrites the legend. It's rather easy to create a sleek narrative where every move fits perfectly into the story. But you would be surprised to see how much of that is often scripted after the fact. Most start-ups go through many painful iterations before finding the right formula.

Speaking of which, it's time for me to share my passion for the HBO series *Silicon Valley*. For outsiders, the script seems like a far-fetched farce written only to make the viewer laugh. But for insiders, the situations depicted in the series are strangely familiar, which makes the stories quite delightful. Of course, this series naturally includes the pivot scene. It's a classic moment that brings back a flood of memories to start-up entrepreneurs. The heroes, the geeks who want to perfect an amazing data compression algorithm, realize they are cornered. Their main competitor has released a version that is better than theirs in every way. They have one day to pivot. The team's business leader initiates a frantic brainstorming session, imagining the most insane concepts, such as an application for tracking children by GPS when they leave school. Incidentally, if you are a highly stressed parent, there are actually loads of real start-ups offering this exact application.

There is no success without one's share of mistakes. Everyone knows that mistakes are often an integral part of an entrepreneur's career. In fact, there is even a famous business conference called FailCon that defines itself as a place for start-up founders to learn from and prepare for failure. Doesn't that sound like a glamorous theme? Actually, the idea is truly interesting. For its first French version in 2012, FailCon asked me to testify onstage.

"You want me to describe all the roadblocks I've been through?" I asked, laughing. "There's plenty to say." I wasn't exaggerating. At Criteo, we tested out nearly every possible way to fail. For the occasion, I made a PowerPoint presentation divided into three chapters:

1. A wrong idea, poorly implemented.
2. A wrong idea, effectively implemented.
3. The right idea, poorly implemented.

It was pretty strange to stand onstage explaining all the mistakes I had made. But this public introspection and formal articulation of my failures was rather instructive, a bit like some kind of business psychotherapy. Here is how it went.

Failure Number One: Wrong Idea, Poorly Implemented

As I previously explained, we had started with a movie-recommendation system. In practice, we had a website that allowed people to rate films and get personalized recommendations. The design was slick, the technology innovative, and the results pretty relevant. Everything was going beautifully—except that our traffic was tiny. In other words, we had all the trouble in the world attracting visitors to our site and getting them to engage with our incredible algorithm.

After a couple of months like this, I started to get very edgy. Our traffic was stagnating at five hundred visitors per day. There was no sign of word-of-mouth growth. We bought advertising on Google to boost our stats, but in vain. The few people who clicked on our ads left the site almost immediately. It was depressing.

The advantage of this first kind of failure is that you can't lie to yourself for long. We didn't need much discussion to agree: we were heading straight for disaster. We realized very quickly that we had to change our model to survive. And that's how we pivoted the first time.

Failure Number Two: Wrong Idea, Effectively Implemented

We remained convinced—and the future would prove us right—that we had a cutting-edge technology around our predictive algorithm. But we needed to know what to do with it. At the time, business-to-business, or B2B, concepts were all the rage. Maybe rather than going directly to consumers, we just had to sell our great technology to other companies. We hadn't gotten very far with our new strategy when our decision to pivot already produced a concrete result. This B2B approach allowed us to smoothly close our series A with investors seduced by our new vision.

Since we hadn't managed to reach movie lovers directly, we decided to go find them where they were. We ended up making a deal with AlloCiné, which is the French equivalent of IMDb. This first contract took several months of difficult negotiations. But through persistence, we eventually secured the contract. Getting our first client was a big moment for the team. As we were about to celebrate with a glass of champagne, I took Cyril, our energetic sales rep, aside and asked him, "Remind me how much we're charging AlloCiné for this contract?"

"Five thousand euros per month. That makes sixty thousand euros per year."

"Sure. But since there are just so many AlloCinés in the world, I'm afraid it will bring us nowhere."

I can still remember how disappointed he looked. It was a little brutal on my part to ruin the party like that. I have very little tolerance for cognitive dissonance, which usually makes me speak my mind too abruptly. But to really scale, it was obvious that we would have to dramatically expand our addressable market. Luckily, my cofounders Franck and Romain were never afraid of new challenges. That was a tremendous difference from my first chief technology officer at Kiwee, whom we had nicknamed "Mr. No" because the mere mention of altering so much as a pixel on our website made him scream that it was simply impossible.

"Impossible" was not a word in Franck and Romain's vocabulary. They reworked the algorithm so that we were able to make recommendations not only for movies but for any product sold online. This was a big improvement. Our young sales team worked like mad again. We quickly convinced half a dozen French online retailers to use our on-site product recommendation solution. By the sweat of our brow, we were finally seeing some revenues. It was just a few thousand dollars per account, but it was encouraging. We could certainly convince other clients. But something was gnawing at me. I felt like I was trying to nail Jell-O to the wall. What was the issue? I didn't exactly know. Or maybe I did.

Deep inside, it was hard to articulate our unique selling proposition. The technology we were offering certainly worked well. Metrics were good, clients agreed. But many clients also thought that they could develop the same tools internally without us. This was causing a lot of friction in the model and did not bode well for the future.

Little by little, I started to get the feeling that we were in the worst of the failure situations: the bad idea decently implemented. I was leading the team down a mediocre path. Of course, with this model, we would undoubtedly be able to do okay, but that's all. A little voice in my head said that I hadn't created a new start-up to do a second Kiwee. I had to set my sights higher, a lot higher. After several months of this slow growth, we had a crisis meeting with the entire executive team.

"We are signing three or four new clients per month and billing them on average $3,000 per month. Extrapolating from this trend, it will take us five years to reach $10 million in revenues," I said.

"In the States, we have a couple of competitors with $20 million in revenue," someone objected.

"I know. I met them," I answered, thinking about the scouting missions I took every year to see how the market was evolving there. "But I'm not envious of those US companies. Ten or twenty million is the same thing. They are just small fishes in a small pond."

"We just have to hang in there. Our clients love us. It's going to take off sooner or later," said Cyril, whose pugnacity in times of crisis always impressed me. But unfortunately, persistence sometimes isn't enough.

"We have an incredible technology. It would really be sad not to find a way to truly leverage it. We just have to find a better way to sell it," I answered.

Franck and Romain were 100 percent aligned with me. They were both obsessed with one thing: how to roll out their magnificent algorithm as widely as possible. Romain often said, "The more the business grows, the more intense our personal experience will be." More than any financial home run, that was what really motivated him.

"What would be great is something you could install in a couple of clicks, a sort of recommendation widget," said Romain, who had deep knowledge of the digital ecosystem.

Geeks have their own code, which can sometimes be hard for outsiders to understand. Widgets are small applications that can be easily installed on any website or blog. At the time, we were smack in the middle of Internet 2.0 fever, which later became what we know today as the social web. Internet users were creating content exponentially, spread over an incessantly growing number of sites. The web had become so rich that there was a growing need for tools capable of offering a personalized selection of pages so that anyone could quickly find what he or she was interested in. Instead of offering personalized product recommendations, we could just as easily recommend blog articles.

The idea was enticing, but I didn't have a very clear idea of how much work it would take to adapt our technical platform to this new challenge. Our cash position from our first round was quickly diminishing. I glanced quizzically at Franck, the algorithm master. His opinion was critical.

As is often the case when he is confronted with a difficult problem, Franck took a few seconds before answering. He calmly considered things, and then he spoke. "I don't see anything preventing us from it. It will take one month, two months max. Actually, we should be able to adapt the algorithm pretty easily."

Easily! I loved it when Franck told us something was easy. Only two months: it was perfect. Franck and Romain never stopped amazing me. Every day, I realized what incredible luck I'd had in encountering these two rare gems in the Parisian incubator after my failed interview with those angel investors.

They got to work along with their small team of developers, for whom the technical challenge was rather exciting. For our sales team, on the other hand, which had succeeded in convincing thirty clients to use our on-site product-recommendation system, it was more complicated. It wasn't easy for them to see us head in a new direction. But I was persuaded that we absolutely needed to try; we needed to pivot one more time and try to finally land something big. And so Criteo set off at full speed for its next destination: failure number three.

Failure Number Three: The Right Idea, Poorly Implemented

It was already the second time in two years we'd had to pivot, and it was a radical change. Not only were we changing audiences—we were no longer addressing e-commerce sites, but bloggers—but the business model was entirely different. To be precise, there wasn't any business model at all. We had simply decided to distribute our widget to bloggers for free. What we wanted above all else was to see our technology operate at scale. We were finally going to find out what our beloved algorithm could achieve with massive data to crunch.

It immediately took off. In no time, thousands of bloggers installed our recommendation widget. After all our time in the wilderness, this success was very gratifying. Seeing our tool spreading like wildfire over the web was so intoxicating.

But we had a little problem. We couldn't come up with a credible business model. And without a way to make money, there would inevitably be a moment when the grim financial reality set in. We were in a typical situation three: a good idea (since our product was a tremendous success with bloggers) poorly implemented (given that it remained economically nonviable). A few years later, Outbrain and Taboola, two Israeli start-ups, proved that with the right approach, content recommendation could indeed become an interesting business.

For us, this experience nevertheless gave us invaluable insight into the browsing patterns of people. We had the intuition that this data could be precious. We just had to figure out how.

Every month, I kept sending the results of our new strategy to our board of directors. Though the traffic figures looked impressive, our revenues stubbornly remained at zero. One month, I remember that this key revenue line miraculously showed a 3. My investors were thrilled.

At the next board meeting, my lead investor, Benoist, said to me, "I saw the figures you sent us. JB, it looks like it's starting to take off. That three on the top line, what does that mean—$3,000?"

"Um …"

"Thirty thousand? Even better!"

"No, it's actually $3. We did $3 in revenues this month."

I remember the look on Benoist's face. Three dollars of revenues for $3 million in fundraising. At least the figure was a round number. Years later, when Criteo became successful, it became a joke between us: Criteo, the start-up that earned $3. But back then, even if I tried my best not to show it, I felt awful.

"I don't see where you're going," Benoist insisted. "JB, what's your plan here?"

"We have tons of traffic. We just need a little more time to find the right business model. This requires fresh money. Given our cash burn, we're going to have to close a new round of financing by the end of the year."

My investors just sighed. There was no need to be a psychic to realize that they were rather skeptical about our chances of success. Then Benoist said to me, "Maybe we should think of doing a bridge?"

My heart skipped. A bridge? I'd rather die! This is where the reader wonders, *What is he talking about?* "Bridge" is investor code for punishing founders for their lack of results. Concretely, the existing investors agree to put a little more money into the company so that it can continue to operate. But this halfhearted support comes with drastic conditions, typically a lower valuation and some additional tight restrictions. In other words, a bridge is usually a founder's nightmare.

I stubbornly continued, "We aren't at that point. We have an amazing tech and a great team. I'm going to look for an outside investor—international, if possible. We just need to tweak our story a bit."

By turning down this bridge and setting off on a round of classic fundraising, I knew I was taking a big risk. If the fundraising didn't go as planned, I was going to find myself with my back to the wall.

At this critical moment, Gilles, who was our only independent director at that time, stepped in. Independent directors have a delicate job. They are generally recruited for their functional expertise and sometime their precious Rolodex. It's clear that they are not there to manage the company, which is the job of the executive team. Nevertheless, the smartest directors are the ones who are able to ask the right questions that will gently push the management out of its comfort zone—which from time to time triggers dazzling insight that changes the course of history.

Having run several software companies himself, Gilles empathized strongly with entrepreneurs and understood the situation better than anyone. But Gilles was also blessed with an essential quality: he was highly benevolent. It may seem incongruous to mention this personality trait when a board of directors requires, above all, professionalism and expertise. And yet I am convinced that a board of directors needs positive personalities in order to function well. The reason is that there is no hierarchy on a board. The directors are, by definition, independent from the CEO. So decision making is naturally collective. In theory, decisions are ratified by a show of hands. In practice, decisions are mostly taken by consensus. In the over fifteen years during which I have been involved in board of directors meetings, I have never witnessed a decision that wasn't reached unanimously. Of course, this does not preclude animated discussions during board meetings, with sometimes long and intense debates. But the precise goal of these discussions is to find common ground. For the board to get there, team spirit is absolutely critical. Jim Warner, our lead director today, is one of those amazing personalities who are so clever at finding the right balance between positive thinking and gentle rigor in our board. That skill is so precious.

Getting back to Gilles, though he came from the world of software and not the Internet, he was a brilliantly intuitive person, like many entrepreneurs. As I was engaged in this tense conversation about a bridge, he suddenly said to me, and almost to everyone in the room, "JB, have you thought of using your algorithm for advertising?"

At the time, I didn't really understand what he meant. And I admit that I listened to him distractedly. Advertising seemed very far from our recommendation algorithm. Gilles's idea appeared destined for the cemetery of lame concepts.

I had no idea that his little question would be the thing that would rescue us from failure number three before it could kill us and that would lead us to finally pivot toward the right thing: our holy grail.

The Light at the End of the Tunnel

Good ideas mature like good wine, slowly. Pivoting to advertising? After all, why not? The more time went by, the more I thought about Gilles's idea. Franck, Romain, and I began brainstorming at the whiteboard. What if we could help our retail customers not directly on their websites but with their advertising spending? There was a lot of money at stake in this area. We started to think of different models, and I could picture some enticing ideas. By analyzing browsing history, our technology had the ability to subtly capture people's shopping intent. With the right approach, there should be interesting ways to create value from this data.

Of course, there is a huge gap between an abstract idea and a fully functioning product. We tried different things for several months. At the end of 2007, we still didn't have a shadow of a real client in advertising, and our new approach was really working only on my PowerPoint slides. It was starting to get very stressful. For lack of anything better, our sales team continued to sell our old on-site recommendation product, but with the same mitigated success. We were starting to see the end of the $3 million from our series A. We had to raise more money quickly, before becoming totally cash-strapped. At this point in the life of a start-up, it's make-or-break time. This typical two-year point, so often fatal, was going to be particularly tough for us to negotiate. We could tell that our existing VCs weren't far from writing us off as losses. The dream team had become a loser team. Seduce new investors? For the moment, we only had a concept that had never been applied anywhere, and we were struggling to prove its worth with numbers. You basically had to be seriously crazy to believe in us.

It Was About Time to Get Lucky

Sometimes fate or chance steps in when needed. As all doors were closing and we were going from an attractive start-up to invest in to a rotten start-up to avoid, I met someone in the United Kingdom who would change Criteo's future. Dominique Vidal, or Dom, was a Frenchman living in London. He had the distinction of being a former entrepreneur, which unfortunately is an exception in the European venture capitalism landscape, where most players have pure finance backgrounds. Kelkoo, his iconic start-up, had been purchased by Yahoo! in 2004. After running Yahoo! Europe for a few years, Dom had just joined Index Ventures, one of the most respected venture capital firms in Europe. Dom was curious, brilliant, and very analytical, and he loved intellectual challenges. When I met him, he immediately understood what we wanted to do. At Kelkoo, he had fought to impose a pay-per-click advertising model on the market, similar to what we were considering.

After preliminary discussions, Dom had me meet his boss. I remember that breakfast in a chic restaurant in central London like it was yesterday, sitting opposite this wildcat of venture capital, who stared at me with his wily eyes, ready to pounce on me for the slightest misstep.

In a tone barely warmer than an iceberg adrift in the polar circle, he asked me, "So where are you with this new advertising model Dom told me about?"

"We're still in a preliminary phase. But our blog-recommendation widget keeps expanding like crazy. It's a great case study of how powerful our engine—"

"But not of how to make money," he said, interrupting me. "I frankly don't understand how you're going to stand out from the crowd. What's so special about your technology anyway?"

This was the crucial, chilling question. If he didn't believe in the technology, the rest of my pitch wouldn't matter. But on the other hand, I didn't see how I was going to explain the subtleties of our algorithm to him in a simple way. He was a pure financier. At best, the presentation could only bore him. At worst, it would give him a good reason to dismiss me and finish his eggs in peace. I thought as fast as I could about what I could tell him. And then I jumped in feet first with a strength born of despair.

"Last month, our movie-recommendation algorithm was ranked among the very best on the Netflix contest leaderboard. Hundreds of teams around the world tried and failed. That proves we have an awesome technology!"

My nearly pleading reply left him as stone-faced as Yoda. I felt miserable. When we stepped outside, I was perplexed. A few days later, though, Dom called to tell me they had agreed to join as the lead investor. I modestly told myself, *You did it, old boy. You sure did convince that financial bigwig. Watch out—here comes the new Steve Jobs!*

I learned the truth much later. In fact, the big boss thought that Criteo's story was quite, well, unconvincing. But since Dom had just joined his team, the boss decided to let him make his one mistake, meaning invest in Criteo—an educational mistake, of course. There is nothing like making an early small blunder to learn the art of investing. The irony is that Criteo, which should have been a quickly forgotten failure of no consequence, became over time one of Index Ventures' biggest hits. Who told you that venture capital returns were somewhat predictable?

Of course, with the backing of this top-tier fund, which had decided to invest $4 million, our existing shareholders magically cheered up. They eagerly agreed to coinvest an additional $3 million. We had gotten a reprieve. With this fresh $7 million injection, we now had the time and the means to develop our big idea. We just had to prove that our technology could apply to advertising—and on the largest possible scale.

It's Not about Who You Are

4

Where We Take Remedial Classes about Digital Advertising

Everything moves fast in the digital economy. In other words, each digital year is easily the equivalent of five years in the traditional world. In our small way, we felt like we were experiencing a time warp, a bit like the astronauts in the film *Interstellar* who are approaching a black hole and see their time scale changing dramatically from the rest of humanity. Trapped in their temporal bubble, they are caught in a race against time.

For start-ups, everything has to go faster, or you die. In early 2008, we now had the financial means for our ambitions. It was time to move into serious execution and really develop this new advertising model that we had pitched to Index. Not only that, but we also had to do it fast, before others beat us to the market.

One morning, Pascal, my freshly recruited sales director, came to see me in a state of excitement. Pascal had learned the ropes of digital marketplaces at Kelkoo under the benevolent wing of Dom Vidal. The first time I met him, it didn't take me long to realize that he had an outstanding commercial intuition. He said to me, "Yesterday I met a former colleague who works in an advertising company. It was really interesting to learn about his work. But something bugged me during our whole conversation. He kept bragging that he had the best *ad server* in the market."

"What's an ad server?"

"I don't really know," he answered frankly. "But I imagine it must be something quite important. Otherwise, he wouldn't have made such a point of it."

Yes, an ad server must be important in the sector we were coveting, but I had no clear idea what it was either. So I quickly Googled the topic. Search engines are amazing. After a few keystrokes, Google can provide us with everything from string theory basics to the chemical compounds of hallucinogenic mushrooms to Freud's semantics. On ad servers, there were thousands of entries. I quickly found heaps of information: an ad server was software used to communicate with websites you want to buy advertising inventory from. In short, it was a core building block if you wanted to get seriously into Internet advertising.

This is a typical problem when you pivot to a business you know very little about. Just to get up to speed, it takes a hefty remedial class on things that are obvious to insiders. I was like a baker who didn't know what flour was.

With my newfound knowledge, I went straight to Romain. I gave him the links I had found on ad servers. His mission was to dig into the matter and see how we could build our own ad server. As usual, he didn't seem intimidated by the task. My two cofounders always impressed me with their technical mastery.

Three months later, everything was ready. We had a platform that would allow those buying advertising to communicate with those selling ad inventory. It was time to have our first "marriage" between a retailer that wanted to increase its revenues through targeted advertising and a publisher that had some unsold display inventory. Criteo would be the technical go-between that allowed this tandem to meet and work together. In fact, we had already found two solid spouses for this proof of concept.

Our First Real Live Case Study

When you are a small start-up in France, it's next to impossible to work with big traditional corporations. Most of them don't even bother picking up the phone. Our only chance was to find a pure player with the right curious mind-set. It happened that during a technology event, I met the founder of a French secondhand online marketplace called PriceMinister, which was offering consumers the opportunity to resell their Christmas gifts, old books, and other used objects. At that time, the company had good traction in France, but its business model worked on small commissions on the products sold. As a result, PriceMinister had very thin margins and couldn't spend much on advertising. It was especially the case for display advertising, which did not work at all for them. Still, Pierre, the founder, didn't hesitate to give us a shot on this test. He was a curious character and was a bit intrigued to see whether we could help his company fix its issue with display advertising. To be honest, he also probably accepted just to give us a chance to prove ourselves. His own debut, which had taken place in the difficult days following the burst of the Internet bubble, was still fresh in his mind, and he knew very well what it meant to struggle when you launched your product and didn't have any client references.

On the publisher side, we had landed Skyblog, which was at that time the largest French blogging platform. Back in 2008, Facebook hadn't reached world domination of social media yet, and Skyblog was very successful in France, with billions of page views every month. The issue was that Skyblog had a rather mixed bag of teen-based content, too teen-based for advertisers to rush to the site. So despite its massive audience, Skyblog also had massive unsold inventory, which made the company open to working with us.

How did it work in practice? PriceMinister gave us permission to analyze how users navigated its site. By crunching millions of data points, we were able to extrapolate consumer shopping intent in real time. With stunning precision, our technology could predict which specific product a particular user was likely to buy. Books, toys, appliances—online marketplaces such as PriceMinister offer millions of products. Choosing the right product for the right person at the right time is a very hard task. If you have spent time looking at different pairs of Adidas sneakers, is it better to show you the latest Adidas design or rather some fancy Nike shoes? And when you have just purchased a high-end camera from Canon, is it better to suggest a memory card or a carrying case? It was time for the machine-learning engine we had built during all those hard years to show its real value.

When Consumers Start to Truly Engage with Online Display Advertising

So there I was in June 2008, excitedly presenting our first results to our board of directors.

"So, guys, what did you learn from your PriceMinister test?" asked Dom, who by now had been part of the adventure for almost six months.

"The results are interesting," I said vaguely. "We increased click-through rate by 25 percent over standard banner ads ..."

"That's very promising," he said, always positive.

"The problem is that it's not enough to convince Skyblog to sell us their inventory at an interesting price."

A glum silence filled the room. My investors didn't really know what to say. We had disappointed them so often that they were nearly fatalistic.

I continued, "But there's a solution. We realized that if we isolate the 30 percent of consumers we have the most shopping data on, the ones we know best, we manage to generate a much better click-through rate."

"How much? How much?" The interest in the room suddenly intensified.

I waited a few seconds to add to the effect and then blurted, "We multiply click-through rate by five."

The number was so huge that it seemed almost too good to be true. And yet we had checked and double-checked it. The improvement in click-through rate was truly spectacular. With such metrics, we felt that Criteo had the potential to completely disrupt the digital advertising market. It's interesting that the day you have an amazing product, you know it immediately.

We got right to work to confirm that these extraordinary results weren't simply the fruit of a lucky combination of circumstances. We started to apply this model very quickly to other online retailers. It worked beautifully. Each time, the click-through rate was far higher than our clients had ever seen before. We started to get large publishers to sell us their inventory too. Each new publisher enlisted reinforced the value of our solution for our clients. It was a truly virtuous circle.

Is Targeted Advertising Creepy?

Traditional online and offline advertising is to a large extent about bombarding random users with random offers, to the point that it has generated what experts call advertising blindness. People don't notice ads anymore; they are just visual pollution. On the contrary, highly targeted ads are very noticeable. We quickly discovered that the supposed indifference people have for banner ads is a myth. If you show consumers the right product at the right time, they will start engaging massively with these offers. Not only do they click on the banners; they will also massively buy those products. What better proof of consumer appetite for targeted ads than those millions of highly engaged clicks every day on our display banners?

Still, I've heard the criticism. Some people accused us of being the new digital Big Brother, spying on people's every move. I completely understand such reactions. According to opinion polls, people generally say they are very protective of their private lives. That's normal, and I'm the same. But these claims actually seem rather paradoxical when you consider how enthusiastically many people post sensitive aspects of their personal lives to Facebook, Twitter, or Google+ with very limited control over who accesses that information. Revelations about certain NSA practices have also fed into a legitimate suspicion of the growing spying on Internet users around the world.

From the start of Criteo, we have taken the subject of privacy very seriously. First of all, a fundamental aspect of our approach is to work only with nonpersonal information. Yes, because this point is very important, I will repeat that all data we collect is anonymous. Not only do we not have any technical means to find users' true identity as they surf the Internet, but we also have no desire to head in this direction. What we are trying to understand is individual *shopping intent* and nothing else. Such things as a person's name, age, and gender are of little use in predicting whether tomorrow that person is more likely to buy a new phone or a pair of shoes.

Dealing only with nonpersonal information was a good start. But very early on in Criteo's history, we wanted to go much farther.

In the spring of 2009, we had one hundred clients, and our service was expanding rapidly. Internet users were clicking on our ads and, better yet, were buying products from our e-merchants. Everything was basically working perfectly. But there was a tiny note of discord. One of our sales rep alerted me to certain complaints registered with customer service. Some users felt they were being secretly spied on. This immediately alarmed me.

We started to answer each complaint by e-mail. We offered to delete all data of users who requested it and, of course, make sure they weren't targeted in the future. But this reactive solution was not enough.

I wanted to go farther. There couldn't be the slightest suspicion of the service being compulsory. We decided to give users the means to decide for themselves whether or not they wished to be targeted. How? In each banner ad, we added a clearly visible button. By clicking on it, users could see all of the data collected and recommendations induced by the engine, with the option to delete everything in one click and stop any future targeting.

At first, many of our clients were reluctant about this new feature. They thought the product was working well, so why make life difficult? If all consumers started to refuse targeted advertising, that would spell the end of this new marketing channel that was so effective. But we held in there. Long-term sustainability of the product was more important to us than any short-term financial gain. And to ensure sustainability, it was key to get the full support of the consumers.

The future proved we were right. The vast majority of users prefer seeing ads that speak to them rather than random irrelevant offers. Quite often, we help them discover cool products they have not previously thought of. And for the small minority who truly prefer random ads for whatever reason, we respect that preference and have given them the option to opt-out in one click.

In this process we discovered something crucial. Most people are not against advertising; they are against *bad* advertising. Well-targeted advertising is welcomed by shoppers because it truly helps them in their buying decisions. Overall, our objective is for advertising to be seen not as a visual nuisance, but rather as an added-value service. In other words, we have aimed to transform advertising into a relevant user experience.

Disrupting the Legacy Business Model

Our ability to offer highly targeted ads was just the tip of the iceberg. The reason we were able to disrupt the market so effectively in the following years came from a major innovation on the business model. This innovation was immediately welcomed by our clients and was a big contributor to our early successes. But even more importantly, it would have profound long-term consequences not only on our go-to market but also on how we ran the company deep inside. I'll come back to that.

Advertising is a huge and rather fascinating industry. Billions are spent every day on campaigns with surprisingly little accountability. Most of the time, financial return on ad spending is based on crude models that, at best, give a very approximate view of what really happened. It's not that advertisers are foolish or reckless. They just don't have the right tools to measure things accurately, so their only choice is to invest blindly and hope for the best.

Ultimately, advertising is always about driving sales. The issue is that the link between advertising spending and revenues is often not that clear. With so much money at stake, a lot of effort has been put into this measurement issue. Unfortunately, this issue is a hard one and is still today the main limiting factor in the advertising industry. All marketing executives dream of the perfect solution that will eventually make their job a science rather than what is today often perceived as some kind of voodoo art.

Working mostly with online retailers in the beginning, we were able to analyze in real time all transactions that took place on their websites. This very granular shopping history was not only precious in figuring out what next product each specific consumer might be interested in. It also gave us the amazing ability to measure in real time the precise impact of all advertising we were doing on clients' behalf. Suddenly, we could offer our clients a model where they would pay only for actual sales leads. In other words, rather than paying for each ad impression, our clients would pay us only when a user actually clicked on a display banner and went to the client's website. What better way to align our interests with those of our clients? Furthermore, clients were already educated on this powerful cost-per-click (CPC) model because of Google, which had used it to scale its massive sponsored-link business.

However, in display advertising in 2008, we were the first company to offer this CPC model to our clients in such a systematic way. Disrupting the cozy display-ad market was so exciting for us. All other players were still offering mainly a cost-per-impression model (called CPM by insiders), where clients were charged no matter what for each ad impression served.

Our luck was that this CPM model was broken in many ways, which created an opportunity to change the game. This element has been core to our success and requires now going a little deeper into how digital advertising works.

The main issue all advertisers face can be summarized in a simple question: am I really getting what I am paying for? To answer this, it's useful to explain that the quality of ad-display inventory relies on four key parameters: the audience (who is looking at the ad), the placement (where the ad is located on the page), the context (what is surrounding the ad), and the format (the shape and size of the ad). In theory, digital ad inventory is supposed to be priced according to its intrinsic quality. However, the market is far from efficient, and for the same price, quality can vary quite a bit. Unfortunately, advertisers' ability to verify audience, placement, and context of the ad is very limited. Advertisers find it almost impossible to ensure they pay the right price for each impression. Their only choice usually is to pay an average price for all impressions bought, which is highly inefficient. To guarantee a certain level of quality, they often try to restrict the buy to easy-to-verify premium ad inventory. However, because competition for this tier-one inventory is very high, it comes with a huge premium on price per impression. In the end, the decision for the advertiser is between high uncertainty and high prices: two bad choices.

The immediate consequence of this lack of visibility in quality is that it is very hard to compute the actual financial value of each ad impression. Some impressions might have a lot of impact, whereas others might be completely useless. Unfortunately, most tracking software has no way to know where the ad is positioned and automatically attributes the same weight to all impressions, regardless of their actual quality. This creates a very serious limitation on how brands can measure financial return on ad spending, to say nothing of potential fraud issues.

To make matters even worse, advertisers also have to worry about what is the optimal number of impressions per user. And this is another difficult problem. The challenge is that beyond a certain number of impressions, the impact of advertising diminishes drastically and could even become negative at some point. As we know intuitively, too much advertising kills advertising. So how do advertisers set the right limit? In practice, this decision is pretty arbitrary, and advertisers just cap the number of ad impressions that a consumer can be exposed to every day. This crude approach overlooks the fact that not all consumers are the same. As a result, some consumers will receive too many ad impressions whereas others will remain underexposed. Overall, this arbitrary capping creates further inefficiencies in companies' buying of ads.

Our clients elegantly solve all those difficult issues by simply switching to our CPC model. It's easy to understand that highly visible banner ads shown to the right audience at the right time have a much higher click-through rate than those ads randomly buried down in the site. A

CPC model automatically adjusts the price of each impression, depending on the actual quality. And interestingly, it does not mean that an impression without any click has no value. CPC is just a powerful mechanism to guarantee that each impression will be paid at the right price. In other words, by paying per click, our clients have a guarantee that they will never overpay for any impression. Furthermore, for each new impression shown to a user, the likelihood of engagement tends to decline. Given this fast-diminishing click-through rate, our engine automatically caps the number of impressions per user at the most optimal level—and ensures that advertisers are not overinvesting in wasteful impressions. In short, the CPC model solves nicely the capping setup issue. Last but not least, CPC pricing makes measuring the return on ad spending much easier. Getting a user to interrupt his or her browsing to click on a banner ad is a rare event, so it is an incredibly strong signal. Multiple studies have shown that clickers are more likely than nonclickers to engage with brands and ultimately buy. Again, this doesn't mean that ad impressions without clicks don't have any value. Clicks simply have much more value.

Of course, this innovative CPC business model did not rub everyone the right way. Some players didn't accept our new way of doing business. In one case I was patiently explaining our approach to an industry veteran who was fifteen years older than I was. I immediately felt some hostility.

"Advertising is first and foremost a tool that has to act on the subconscious," he said to me in a slightly professorial tone. "Our job is to influence consumers over the long term. And for that, the click-through rate is highly irrelevant. It's a well-known fact that people who click never buy. Your CPC business model just incentivizes you to send as many clicks as possible to your clients to overcharge them."

I could sense that he was getting angry as he spoke. I responded as calmly as possible. "We don't just look at clicks. Our goal is also to convert the maximum number of clicks into actual purchases. And that's what happens. Our clients confirm this every day."

"Anyway, people who click on banner ads are losers," he said tersely.

I was so flabbergasted that I couldn't speak. In a way, this type of hostility is quite telling. Some incumbents have a vested interest in things not changing. Let me explain why.

Ultimately, the only thing that matters to advertisers is how much return they are really getting for their money. To calculate this financial return on ad spending, typically you choose a metric and measure the impact of the display ads on this metric. For example, with a retail or travel website, you would measure direct sales generated from display ads, or more specifically, visits generated by those ads and the related conversions into sales. For other verticals such as automotive, conversions can be a test drive, an application submission, or another industry-specific relevant business metric.

Once the metric is defined, you need to decide when and how to attribute a conversion to the specific ad campaign. This is the point where things become more complicated. There are fundamentally two scenarios that bring a user who has been exposed to a banner display ad to your website and that ultimately generate a conversion:

- Direct, where a user follows a click on a banner display ad. This is called a click-through (or postclick) conversion.
- Indirect, where the user decides on his own to visit the website. This is called a view-through (or postview) conversion.

Click-through conversions have no issues. As we said, getting consumers to willingly interrupt their browsing to click on a banner ad is incredibly hard. As a result, when someone does so, it's a very strong and well-accepted marketing signal. Furthermore, it's very easy to control quality of click-through conversions. You just have to monitor conversions of those incoming postclick visits during a predefined attribution window (typically thirty days). This has been done at scale for years on search marketing campaigns. As a result, advertisers are usually very quick to spot the difference between high-quality clicks generating strong postclick conversions and poor-click channels that need to be eliminated from the marketing mix. The implicit assumption of a CPC pricing model is that only click-through conversions should be taken into account for the calculation of the return on ad spending. This is why our CPC model is becoming so popular among advertisers; it makes both quality control and calculation of return on ad spending so easy.

The challenge is that showing an attractive return on ad spending with pure click-through attribution is very hard. In fact, we were the first service provider capable of offering this model in a scalable way. For others who are struggling to emulate our model, it's very tempting to add to the mix some view-through conversions on top of the click-through conversions. Suddenly, the ROI looks so much better! View-through conversions are based on the idea that a banner ad impression has "influenced" the user, causing him or her to visit the website at a later time. View-through attribution gives banner ad campaigns some credit for those conversions.

This is where things get messy. How do you know whether a particular user was truly influenced by an ad impression or just visited the site for another reason?

In practice, there is no way to make this distinction. View-through advocates try to circumvent this issue by asking for a very conservative attribution window. For instance, whereas click-through conversions typically have a thirty-day window, view-through conversions may be measured during a twenty-four-hour window or even just a few hours. This tight attribution window looks very attractive at first glance, but in reality, even a small view-through window can completely distort the calculation of return on ad spending.

To explain why, we need to go back to a little secret of the advertising industry: a very large fraction of the banner ad inventory is in fact below the fold (more than 70 percent of impressions are not visible on certain networks). Those impressions are very cheap to buy, precisely because almost nobody sees them.

To artificially boost view-through conversions, you just need to buy large amounts of those very cheap below-the-fold impressions. Users won't see them, but who cares? The cost is minimal, and the point is to simply drop a tracking cookie for each of those impressions and then claim credit for any conversion later. This is what experts call "cookie stuffing." Unfortunately, some advertisers are still unaware of this dirty trick—and even when you are aware, it's very hard to prevent—which makes this technique even more tempting for some unscrupulous service providers. The danger is ending up with a massive number of illegitimate conversions wrongly attributed to the ad campaign: great return in appearance, but in reality a complete waste of money.

Ultimately, the only way to measure the precise uplift of display ads is to run a statistically significant and valid A/B test where you expose only one group to your display ads and you then measure the difference in results. To avoid any sample biases, A/B tests require a very tight protocol, as rigorous as that implemented for drug trials. We've run hundreds of these A/B tests for our clients, and experience has shown that on average, incremental revenue uplift is around 20 percent higher than when only click-through conversions are taken into account. In other words, the click-through model is a very solid and safe proxy for true incremental value.

In short, CPC is a simple and transparent business model that guarantees that clients always pay the right price. Nevertheless, when we launched our product in 2008, many advertisers were easily fooled by CPM pricing with shiny view-through attribution models. It took us quite some time to get them to measure things in a more rigorous way. The funny thing in hindsight is that the reason we came out with such a disruptive model was probably because we did not come from the advertising industry. With fresh eyes and no legacy business to protect, it's a little easier to think outside the box.

A Virtuous Business Model Not Only for Our Clients, but Also for Us

During the fall of 2008, we managed to convince dozens of online retailers to use our solution. Word of mouth was picking up, and our sales team was getting increasingly busy and excited.

Very quickly, we came up against another problem: what advertiser should we pick for a consumer who was interested in a multitude of very different products at the same time (which is pretty much all of us)? In other words, when Expedia, Macy's, and Sears all have an offer relevant for a particular prospect, which of the three should get the ad impression on the publisher website? The solution was a real-time auction, where each ad impression was awarded to the highest bidder, the client of ours ready to pay the most for this particular person in this specific context. This model was mainstream in the search marketing world but still very new in the display advertising world.

At this stage, it's worth saying a word on how we buy advertising. This buying side is usually not well understood by people outside our industry. Nevertheless, it's a key element of our business.

Remember that we charge clients only if a consumer clicks on a banner. Well, no matter what, Criteo still has to pay publishers for all ad impressions we purchase. This means that, de facto, we lose money on all impressions that do not generate clicks. The consequence is that in order for us to make money, we need to be able to accurately predict in a particular context the likelihood that a consumer will click on a banner ad and buy. In other words, our job is to predict in real time whether or not someone will engage with a specific ad impression. There are potentially hundreds of parameters that can influence that. For example, what time of day is it? The morning is the most suitable for smartphones, daytime is best for desktop computers, and we notice a strong increase in tablets in the evening. What day of the week is it? The weekend is much more important in Europe than in the United States. What content is the user looking at? On social networks, where you are interacting with friends and family, you are generally less receptive to advertising. On the contrary, on a news website, the user's mind is more inclined to discover new products. Even the weather has an important impact on our activity. At Criteo, we love rainy days because people spend more time in front of their screens and buy more online.

This prediction problem is a hard one. But it had two very interesting consequences for Criteo. First, if you can solve a hard technical problem that has a lot of value for your clients, this creates a serious barrier to entry for future competition. We'll come back to that. Second, any improvement in our predictive technology has a direct positive and immediate impact on our revenues.

This second aspect has proved crucial in how we've managed our product road map. Over the years, product road maps are indeed one of the most difficult processes in any technology company. The reason is that there are always more ideas than software developers available. So for each new cool feature you add, you need to evaluate carefully what the impact on revenues will be. This is usually a very difficult exercise because the two things (product features and revenues) are only loosely connected to each other. But not in our case—each time we have a new idea, we just have to answer one simple question: does this improve or not our ability to predict whether a consumer is going to buy? This question has made product choices so much easier. And it creates powerful alignment of our teams on common objectives. As we started to expand very quickly in people and locations, the risk of losing focus was very high, with initiatives going in too many different directions. Thanks to our particular business model that created this natural alignment, we probably suffered much less from this issue than many other fast-growing tech start-ups.

It's Not about Who You Are, but What You Want

When mass production first appeared, pioneers also invented mass advertising. The game was to define typical groups of consumers, such as the Coca-Cola teenager or the Heinz family. Individuals existed only as part of a target audience. However, at any given instant, people who appear to be very similar are interested in very different things. And very different people want to buy the same thing.

We can now offer a new way to approach advertising. Instead of targeting people based on what they *are* (their age, gender, home address, or marital status), we concentrate on what they *want* (a new phone, a sofa, a beach vacation, etc.). In the world of advertising, it's a surprisingly revolutionary concept. To make this happen, two key ingredients are necessary: the ability to capture shopping intent and the ability to measure sales in real time.

For a long time, it was next to impossible to capture precise shopping intent at the user level. Thanks to the fast digitalization of the world, it's now becoming increasingly possible. It all started with people typing keywords into search engines. Suddenly, millions of consumers were indicating in real time which particular product or service they were interested in. Google made gold with this data and in less than ten years has become the most powerful advertising company in the world. Thanks to sophisticated machine-learning technologies, Criteo has applied this idea to other types of consumer data: digital purchase history, online shopping carts, and other high-value desktop and mobile browsing signals. We can now accurately extrapolate high-quality shopping intent in more and more marketing scenarios.

At the other end of the value chain, we've seen that it has been historically very challenging for advertisers to precisely link their advertising investments with their revenues. Thanks to breakthrough technologies, it's now increasingly possible to make this link not only with perfect precision for each consumer but also in real time. This ability to close the loop allows us to optimize media buying in a way that was just impossible to dream of before.

We are still only at the very start of these massive changes driven by the growing, ubiquitous presence of the digital world in our lives. The multiple consequences are profound and still not well understood by many players in the industry. Above all, these changes mean that the main success factor is no longer relationships but technology. When everything gets measured easily and accurately, your Rolodex does not matter that much anymore. What matters is how good your technology is—because technology is what drives performance. And in the end, the capability to generate actual revenues better than anyone else is what makes you win and keep your clients. This fundamental shift in how value is generated in the industry will dramatically remodel the advertising landscape. Players who aren't able to make this transition to technology will simply disappear.

How quickly this will happen? How long before the geeks completely dominate this space that for so many years was the private preserve of fancy sales reps? Once more, the two key driving forces are the ability to capture shopping intent and the ability to measure impact of advertising in real time and at the user level. As soon as you are able to connect the dots of the consumer marketing journey, technology wins. Expanding our footprint smartly in these two domains is what has been driving the growth of Criteo so far and is fundamentally what will fuel our future growth too. So far, we've captured only a very small fraction of the vast universe of consumer shopping intent. And we've been monitoring only a small fraction of all retail sales. There is just so much more we could do. I have to admit that I am fascinated to see how far we can go.

Time for a New Start

For Criteo, the first three years from 2005 to 2008 were really difficult, even a little depressing. We felt like we were banging our heads against the wall without ever finding the right solution. This dark period left a mark on us. We realized how important persistence is for success. Hopefully, this value is now rooted in the company's genes. When the product finally showed its true potential in the summer of 2008, everything suddenly accelerated. By the end of the year, we had started to expand outside of France. Naturally, we started with the countries bordering France: Germany, Italy, and the United Kingdom. We could see some nice traction everywhere. At last, life was getting good, and we could start to relax a bit.

However, in May 2009, we had a board meeting that would set a new course for our story. "With the current momentum, I think we are not going to make our budget," I started to explain.

"Do you mean that Criteo is going to miss its revenue target of $10 million that we set at the start of the year?" asked one of our directors.

Clearly, I was not expressing myself well. But remember—we hadn't really accustomed our investors to outstanding results. So I just relished the effect of my words even more.

"What I mean is that at the rate things are going, we aren't going to do $10 million this year, but $15 million. We are growing very quickly in France. And Germany, the United Kingdom, and Italy are starting to follow the same course. In fact, I'm wondering if now's the right time to go big—really big."

A strange, attentive silence filled the room. Many start-ups encounter this crucial moment in which they have to choose between accelerating or consolidating. In our case, consolidating was out of the question. I didn't see myself cooling things down when everything was pointing in the other direction. I had made my mistake with Kiwee. When all lights are green, it's time to push as if tomorrow will be the last day of your life.

I changed gears: "We are already profitable in Europe with still a lot of growth ahead of us. If we're going to try the US, it's now or never."

The room turned silent again. Given our very rapid growth month after month, my investors were now much more confident in the future of the company—quite a change in mood from eighteen months earlier.

Dom Vidal then spoke to sum up the overall feeling: "We'll support you. And if necessary, we're even ready to increase our funding. But concretely, how do you plan to go about it? Are you going to recruit someone to manage America? Or send someone over there?"

"The US market is far too complex to be managed from a distance. I'll have to go myself. As soon as I get a work visa—which should take around two months—I'll move my family to Silicon Valley."

As you can imagine, this news was a bombshell. This was a major change for the company. My wife and I had talked it over a few days before. Why not go to the States? It wasn't any crazier than starting an organic soup and salad shop. So when I spoke with her about the idea of moving to California, she didn't hesitate. The prospect of allowing our daughters to experience two cultures was very exciting. Furthermore, since my wife was working as a freelancer doing website development, relocating was not an issue for her.

It was more complicated for my investors. They were worried about the impact on Criteo. Being so remote, how would I manage the team in Europe? I explained that I was planning to do round-trips every month. Dom asked me why I wouldn't consider the East Coast. New York was starting to emerge as a meaningful hub in the tech world, and the time difference with France was only six hours. Those three extra hours for California would be so much more painful. I quickly dismissed that option. I wanted to be in the heart of the tech rain forest. All our key partners were over there—Google, Yahoo!, Microsoft, Amazon—as well as Facebook, the new kid on the block everyone was starting to talk about. It was too bad about the nine hours of time difference, but I didn't see myself anywhere but in California.

The deal was done. With my family and four large suitcases, I set off for Silicon Valley. It was double or nothing.

West Side Story 5

Home of the Geeks

"California dreamin' on such a winter's day." The Beach Boys' rendition of this song was running through my mind. I still remember how excited I felt when my family and I landed at the San Francisco airport. It was like starting from scratch in a place where everything seemed possible. You just have to drive on the 101 that crosses Silicon Valley from San Francisco to San Jose to realize that this is a different planet. What struck me the most at first? The gigantic billboards along the freeway that, instead of touting the usual merits of some fancy shampoo, praised computer security routers and cloud-based hosting services: advertising for geeks. After all, what could be more natural in their kingdom?

In Hollywood, everyone seems to be an aspiring actor or has a screenplay to sell. Here in the Bay Area, every Starbucks barista or Uber driver has a business plan on his or her smartphone and dreams of becoming the next Steve Jobs. Yes, you really are in the future here—not only because a disproportionate amount of all-new high-tech products are designed in the region but also for another utterly simple reason. California is practically the last time zone on the planet. I love the feeling of waking up in the morning while the rest of the world has nearly finished its day. I have everything in front of me. Checking my in-box, I can see at a glance all that was thought of, considered, and discussed by our teams in all the time zones working before me. What a chance to benefit from all this collective intelligence to start my day.

First Misadventures in the Valley

In the summer of 2009, I arrived with my family in Silicon Valley as the founder of a start-up that was starting to take off. I couldn't help remembering my very first trip to the Valley ten years earlier. It was in the fall of 1998. Not Facebook or Twitter or even Google was on the map yet. I was twenty-nine years old. As I explained before, a few years before, I had gotten burned by Kallback, my lousy first entrepreneurial gig. By 1998, I had realized that the Internet was the future, and I was obsessed with the idea of making up for lost time in the start-up world. I had negotiated a three-month unpaid leave of absence with my boss and had packed my bags to go discover the Valley, the Kathmandu of all geeks.

What was my plan at that time? My big idea was to convince a cool California start-up to license its technology for Europe. I arrived light-heartedly in San Francisco. With the Internet bubble brewing, the city was already terribly expensive. In order to not eat up too much of the little nest egg that I had struggled to amass over the previous years, I needed the cheapest accommodation possible. I tried my luck with a distant wealthy cousin who was living in an enormous posh house in central San Francisco, but she pretended not to understand. So I ended up in the city's shadiest motel, a shabby ten-dollar-a-night room with nothing more than a wrought iron bed and a bare lightbulb hanging from the ceiling by a cord. For the toilet and shower, I had to line up with the rather sinister-looking lot that called this fleabag home.

But who cares? What mattered was my project. For three months, I crisscrossed the Bay Area searching for that rare gem. My perseverance got me in the door of a few decent local start-ups. But they only half-listened to me, and I was turned away at the end of each meeting. Should this have come as a surprise? I was a total stranger, with no references or credibility. I ended up with nothing, and when my three months were over, I went back to square one in Paris. In France, the Internet fever was growing more by the week. And I had no idea where to start. Then came a warm evening at a café terrace on the Ile Saint-Louis in July 1999. I remember it like it was yesterday. I was having a drink with a friend I hadn't seen in ages. We were discussing business trends, and he told me straight out, "I've just launched a start-up in financial services with three cofounders. In six months, we secured a series A of $2 million. It's gonna be huge."

This felt like a shock to the brain. How had a guy like him, whom I perceived as the typical salary man, managed to start a company and raise so much money so quickly, while I, who called myself an entrepreneur and talked nonstop about my future company, had nothing to show for it? I was furious at myself.

The next morning, I handed my resignation to my boss. I had no idea what I was going to do, but my back was up against the wall. Something was bound to happen. Something had to. And that's how Kiwee, my start-up specializing in ringtones, was born. Kiwee had some early successes, but we never really committed ourselves seriously to expanding outside France. In particular, we never dared to tackle the Everest of any start-up: the United States of America.

The Advantage of Flying under the Radar

Conquering the United States: that's the dream of every start-up founder. The challenge is formidable, particularly for outsiders. How many European Internet companies have succeeded in the US market? Almost none. Despite these less-than-encouraging statistics, we were convinced that it was worth a shot for Criteo. We knew we had a unique product. As strange as it may seem, in 2009 there was no one in the United States doing targeted display advertising with a scalable cost-per-click business model like Criteo. Such an opportunity was worth a shot.

Interestingly, the fact that we had begun our project in France also gave us an unexpected advantage in this race. First of all, France had a pool of highly qualified engineers with strong mathematical skills who were particularly relevant for the type of technology we were building. And those talented engineers came at a fraction of what they cost in Silicon Valley. The second advantage of having started Criteo in Paris was precisely because it was such an unlikely location for a tech venture. In the world of advertising technology, the American leadership is so impressive. Who would ever guess that cutting-edge innovation in this field could come from France, the country of fashion and cheese? This allowed us to quietly grow under the radar for the first few years. On purpose, we didn't do any press releases on our product. The only people who knew about it were our clients. When Criteo suddenly became visible in 2011, we had already reached a critical size that made any copycat attempt much harder.

Palo Alto, the City Cut in Two

In 2009, I came to the Valley not as a broke aspiring entrepreneur anymore but as the founder of a promising tech start-up. What could be more exciting than starting this new adventure? It was almost like creating another start-up inside Criteo. This time, I wasn't going to beg local players to license their cool technology for Europe. This time, it was the Europeans who were bringing breakthrough technology to the American market.

When I had to find our first office space, I didn't hesitate for very long. It would be in Palo Alto, the capital of Silicon Valley. For my family, we had found a nice house that was light-years from my sordid hotel in 1998 (I had a feeling my wife and daughters wouldn't have appreciated it for very long). The house was on the west side of Palo Alto because the real estate agent had told me I didn't have much of a choice for the sake of the girls' schools. On the other hand, when it came to finding an office, I looked for something cheaper. I found just that on the other side of Route 101, at a rock-bottom price, on the east side of Palo Alto. What I didn't know was that East Palo Alto was another world. Not long ago, it held the sad distinction of having one of the highest crime rates in the United States.

Palo Alto is truly a surprising city. It is cut in two by Highway 101. You just have to follow University Avenue, the main road, from west to east. When you cross the 101, you feel like you have stepped through a looking glass.

I took this route every day by bike, a thirty-five-pound Chinese-manufactured cast-iron bike that I had bought for eighty dollars at Walmart and that nearly came to a dead stop anytime I stopped pedaling—a nice metaphor for the life of a start-up, in fact. This daily commute by bike was very educational. On the west side of Palo Alto were the privileged classes, the residential neighborhoods with beautiful tree-lined streets and perfectly manicured lawns, where Steve Jobs and so many mythic tech figures lived. There were the venture capitalists who gathered on Sand Hill Road, the Champs-Elysées of the profession. There were the tech start-ups that filled most of downtown (other than where the VCs roosted). The west side had cozy coffee shops; the legendary Italian restaurant Il Fornaio, where according to the legend, so many deals have been made over a plate of seafood penne, the house specialty; and the ubiquitous Apple Store, the hi-tech cathedral, where Steve Jobs still came in person in 2009 to launch new products. In the street, cars were shiny, sometimes all electric, and people were thin and active. Every terrace table was abuzz with conversations about tech and fundraising, a joyful mix of young geeks in jeans and sneakers rubbing shoulders with graying investors in their impeccable striped shirts. In a still predominantly WASP world, Indians and Chinese held a growing place of importance while a few Europeans did their best to represent the Old World.

On the east side, it was another story. Houses were fenced in, surrounded by wooden barriers. There were frequent burglaries and muggings. The population was very mixed, dominated by Latinos. There were no Apple Stores, but rather small offices that offered wire transfer services to foreign countries. For a long time, people from the west side didn't dare to step foot in the east for fear of being robbed. East Palo Alto was a dodgy area, enough so to surprise some of my investors when they discovered my address.

"JB, are you sure you want to set up shop there? It's a no-go zone!"

Too bad. It was done. I had already signed the lease. Actually, the situation suited me fine. This first office space was absolutely functional, spacious, and filled with light. And I knew that it would be temporary and that we would eventually move, to the good side this time.

Profession? Recruiter

The next step consisted of recruiting my first US team. I was eager to launch our American business as soon as possible. Because I didn't have any local contacts in my Rolodex, I knew I could use some external help. The solution came indirectly from Dom Vidal, who had the art of connecting me to the right experts who could contribute to the business. That is exactly what you should expect from a good venture capitalist. From his time at Yahoo!, Dom had retained a lot of connections. Actually, the mafia of ex-Yahoos is quite impressive and has played an important role in the development of Criteo. Thanks to Dom, we asked one of them, Toby Coppel, to become our new independent director. Toby had started his career as an investment banker and had found himself at a young age managing all of Yahoo's strategic partnerships during the portal's glorious years of high growth. Toby is reserved by nature, which is interestingly an excellent means of making other people speak. It wasn't easy convincing someone who had such a stellar career to join a French start-up that, though quite promising, was still fragile and completely unknown in the United States. Dom put his credibility on the line to convince Toby to join our board.

Because of his experience, Toby was obviously very well connected in Silicon Valley. I naturally turned to him to ask for his guidance about my first baby steps in America.

"I need to find someone to help me build the US team. I'm in discussion with a few headhunters, but I'm not really thrilled with any of them."

"You don't need a headhunter. You need to have someone who works only for you, someone who is dedicated, heart and soul, to Criteo. In other words, the first person you should hire is an in-house recruiter. Every start-up in the Valley has one. As opposed to an external headhunter, an in-house person knows she will then have to work with the new hires. So she will make sure to find you the very best."

I had never heard of such a job. The job title "recruiter" reminded me of military service. "A recruiter? You mean a human resources director?"

"No, it has nothing to do with that. A recruiter is a salesperson more than anything else, someone who will sell the company to talents you want to hire."

And of course Toby knew the perfect candidate for this job. He put me in touch with Margo, a hunter who specialized in top talents. She had worked closely with Toby in the past at Yahoo! This particular connection was necessary to convince this high-flying recruiting expert to take the risk to join a European start-up that was completely unknown in the Valley.

How to Become an American Start-Up with a Few Coats of Paint

Three days after our interview, Margo was in our office. Everything goes so quickly in California that it seems like magic. We got to work immediately. I was obsessed with recruiting a top sales team. I was listing for Margo all of the qualities I wanted in an ideal sales rep when she interrupted me with an engaging smile.

"The first issue we're going to have to face is that Criteo is a French start-up."

"Um, you mean we're going to have a hard time getting Americans to work for a French boss?"

"No, the fact that you're French doesn't matter. Silicon Valley is so cosmopolitan that it's not unusual to see local start-ups with French, German, Indian, or Chinese founders. People are used to it."

"Then what's the problem?"

"We're a foreign start-up that's not local. That's what's going to make things challenging."

Margo had the great merit of being brutally honest. She was obviously right. A European tech start-up didn't mean much in the American imagination, especially in Silicon Valley, where there were all those shiny start-ups on the corner of every street reaching out to you. It was basically like asking Michael Jordan to play on a team from Greece—not impossible in theory, but not likely to happen. Our product was great, and there was a good chance it would work here as well as in Europe. But for that to happen, we had to get the sales machine running. I quickly changed gears.

"Okay. We're going to do everything to make the company look as American as possible. I'm already based here. That's a strong symbol, isn't it?"

"That's the least you could do. If you weren't here, I wouldn't have even considered joining you."

"Even if it's only you and me today, let's make Palo Alto officially our global headquarters. A founder in the States, headquarters in the States ... that's a start."

And that's how we did our little cosmetic surgery. Even if from a strict legal standpoint Criteo's headquarters remained in France, we did everything possible to hide this shameful flaw. On our corporate website, Palo Alto was mentioned as our official headquarters. I went all in on the American angle. On my LinkedIn profile, I tried all I could to insist on my local presence. My daughters went to an American school. I started eating cheeseburgers with ketchup daily. I even tried to learn the rules of baseball, which says a lot.

I also decided to bring local investors into the picture. In a young start-up, the most visible element is often its investors. By choosing a solid US venture capitalist, I would give much more substance to my American story. At that time, we were already break-even and did not need a new cash injection. So I was going to get diluted. But who cared if that was the price to pay to conquer the US market? Margo was thrilled. And that's how we did our third investor round in the spring of 2010 with Bessemer, one of the most respected venture capitalists in Silicon Valley.

And yet despite this plan of action, despite our new American investor, and despite the work of Margo, our high-end recruiter, we had a very hard time hiring during our first two years in the States. The more we searched for seasoned managers, the more challenging it was. No matter what we did to play down the fact that we were of European origin, there remained a sort of negative aura. We remained the company that seemed American but actually wasn't. That was creating friction at each step of our growth. For instance, I had a strong CFO candidate who turned down our offer at the last second because he suddenly realized that the stock options were issued by a French company. His lawyer strongly advised him not to be compensated with such "exotic" securities!

Looking for Our First Whale

To get started, we had to bring over a certain number of Criteo employees from Europe. Obviously, they were all thrilled to stay for a while in California. Working with our freshly recruited US local team, we landed a few second-tier accounts. However, to really give us the credibility we desperately needed, we required one big domestic client. This was no small matter. I remember endless conversations with my young American sales team in which I had to reenergize them so they wouldn't become too depressed. It was just so hard to convince clients to try a non-American technology.

We were going in circles. We didn't have any local references. Our hundreds of European clients didn't count here. Everyone told me the same thing: come back when you can show American case studies. This seemed crazy to me because the Internet worked exactly the same way in Europe as in the United States. But there was nothing to be done.

I was obsessed with a single objective: to land a big local fish, just one, but one that would have symbolic value. Finally, the sales team spotted a real whale: Zappos, the leading online shoe retailer in America. *Shoes?* I thought. It didn't necessarily seem to be the best-suited category to sell on the Internet. And yet in Europe, we had a couple of shoe clients who were doing extremely well. There was no reason we could not reproduce this success in the United States.

Zappos was the ideal reference because its brand was so visible. Furthermore, the company was recognized by its peers for its exceptional focus around customer service and, more generally, user experience. Customer service is like a real religion for its founder, who wrote an entire book on the topic. With such high standards, this target client was quite intimidating for our sales team. But it was exactly what we needed, and after several months of stressful discussions, Zappos agreed to test us. As always, they naturally kept an extremely attentive eye on user experience related to Criteo's highly targeted banners. All of Criteo's technical resources were mobilized to create nearly every look and feel possible. After countless iterations, Zappos' decision makers were finally won over. Criteo's little California team was justifiably proud and began to feel more confident. Once we had landed this key client, everything became easier. Zappos triggered the right word of mouth in the marketing community, and at last, people started answering the phone when we called.

Success begets success—a kind of snowball effect, I would say. Thanks to Zappos and the momentum it created, we were also able to hire people of higher caliber, such as Greg Coleman, the former head of sales of all of Yahoo! He was a legend in the digital advertising world, and joining us was no easy move for him. After several rounds of discussion, we convinced him to become our president. He confided to me that at that time, his wife told him he was making a big mistake. After all, a French start-up doing ad tech? With hindsight and our successful listing on the stock market, I believe she became a big Criteo fan.

Pajama Day at School, American-Style Education

Despite having struggled, I have very fond memories of this period, the heroic conquest of America. So does my family, even if some days were a bit rough. When we arrived, my daughters were five and seven. They didn't speak a word of English, and we dropped them straight into a local school without any preparation. The first six months were a real ordeal, featuring daily combat with this new foreign language that refused to be tamed. Today, I have to fight to get my daughters to answer me in French.

Discovering the American school system was absolutely fascinating. At first, it seemed to be based on polar opposite principles from the European educational system. Even if they can work quite hard, children who come from Europe sometimes feel US schools are like Disneyland. Rather than focusing on academic knowledge, the education system's objective seems indeed to be primarily to give students a sense of confidence. For European parents, this can be a little disconcerting. But I must admit that the approach undoubtedly had a galvanizing effect on the kids. The teachers have rubber stamps marked "Great!" or "Awesome!" and they cover the children's quizzes and tests with them. Seen through the lens of the French system, where it is often difficult to do better than "satisfactory," this appears a little surreal. Not to mention rituals such as Pajama Day, in which everyone, teachers and principal included, wear their pajamas to school. Needless to say, kids love it.

Of course, Americans debate as much about education as Europeans. And as in all developed countries, it's a subject of sharp controversy. For instance, some parents insist on more academic education and severely critique this system that tries to convince children they are all champions. They argue that this new generation will be too pampered and ill-prepared for the future. I have a certain distance from this debate. As an eternal optimist, I believe the blend of European old culture and American positive thinking is a stimulating cocktail for my daughters. In fact, it was quite amusing to see Palo Alto bookstores overloaded with books written by Anglo-Saxon expatriates in Paris who seemed amazed by the manners of French children and the values of tradition and respect we are supposed to instill in them, which I guess just goes to show that the grass is always greener on the other side.

Halloween and the God of Technology

At any rate, my daughters ended up adopting California, big time. Perhaps it was because of Halloween, which never really made it to Europe that much. In Palo Alto, October 31 is madness. Until Steve Jobs's death, the big ritual was to trick-or-treat at his house. His wife was known for decorating her yard with glow-in-the-dark skeletons and all kinds of gory zombies. Legend has it that one of the bags of candy she gave out to children contained an iPhone. Because of that, every year on Halloween night, a huge, joyful crowd of colorful witches, little vampires, and all kinds of ghouls, everyone hoping to be the lucky winner, would gather in front of their home. In the Valley, Steve Jobs was like a God. When he died, the local scene froze for several days. Silent and sad, people left apples and testimonials in front of his house. Apple Stores were in mourning, with large pictures of him on display. There was something almost religious about these acts.

Silicon Valley is really a world unto itself, where God is progress and the core religion is technology. To the outside world, California geeks can come off as dreamers. Their faith is so strong that they are convinced they can "evangelize" the world via technology. Here, gurus are everywhere with far-fetched theories such as Kurzweil's singularity, a hypothetical event in which artificial intelligence would be capable of recursive self-improvement up to the point of an explosion of intelligence beyond anything humans could understand. One of the most creative thinkers regarding the role of technology in our society is Kevin Kelly, whose book *What Technology Wants* has resonated so much in the Valley. His fascinating theory is that technology is actually a living, breathing being. The way he explains this is that if we look over the course of history, technology has evolved in a similar way to humans. Each new technology is the logical consequence of previous technologies that are recombining in new ways. As a result, he speculates that we can fairly accurately predict the macro future evolutions (robots with human-approaching intelligence) but not the details (will they be made of silicone?). His theory is both disturbing and captivating in terms of moral consequences and actual freedom of choice for all the geeks who collectively are building our future.

Did You Say Entrepreneur? 6

French-Bashing Always Sells

Surprisingly, "entrepreneur" is a loanword from French, having come into being in the early eighteen century, a long time ago. Today, France is regularly depicted as the sick country of Europe, the victim of suffocating government control. As one joke puts it, France is the country where communism succeeded. The cute tendency of French elites to drape themselves in principles that we apply only to others and to preach the universalism of a model that has aged in many respects can be quite annoying too.

The time when American multinationals set up their European headquarters in Paris, the geographical center of Western Europe, is long gone. When a US start-up wants to expand to Europe, London is now the most natural beachhead—sometimes Dublin, for tax reasons mainly. Convincing Americans that France isn't just the country of the Eiffel Tower, the Louvre, and castles of the Loire Valley is not easy. When it comes to Internet-related industry, it has to be admitted that although Paris is roughly on par with Berlin, it's definitely less cosmopolitan than London. Is it a question of a linguistic barrier? Not only. I sometimes get the sneaking suspicion that for many US investors, France is only a destination for a romantic, slightly erotic getaway—a sort of delicious, decadent, picturesque world with dreams of faded glory. However, American investors who can go beyond their prejudices are sometime delighted. With Criteo, they even hit the jackpot.

That said, how can you hold a grudge against the Anglo-Saxons when the uncontested champions of French-bashing are the French? And the French-bashers-in-chief are clearly French senior executives. Whether they are running big companies or small businesses, they howl a symphony of jeremiads in unison.

"Labor laws are pushing us to bankruptcy!" "Income tax is killing us!" "A country of bureaucrats always on vacation!" I've heard this same old song forever. It eventually has become an axiom, a truth that no one even bothers contradicting anymore. I admit that I have a hard time identifying with this systematically pessimistic view.

Most Europeans are convinced that they pay much higher taxes than Americans. With a company listed on the Nasdaq and my family living in the United States, I look—in the eyes of my fellow countrymen—like the typical entrepreneur who fled France, that socialist country with ridiculous taxes. However, I am anything but a tax exile. Actually, the fact that I became a California resident significantly increased my income taxes compared to what I would have paid in Europe. Furthermore, in California, stock options are considered to be part of one's income and are logically taxed at the same marginal rate. In the end, it's interesting to point out that taxing capital gains as salary, which in Europe is usually considered absurd, is a well-accepted standard in California, the archetype of tech capitalism. Last, most Europeans have no idea that states such as California tax real estate at 1 percent of face value every year. Needless to say, a similar tax levy in Europe would start a revolution.

The Battle for High-End Immigrants

Quite often, the right experts you need to grow your wonderful start-up are not located in the same city as your headquarters. As a result, the stakes around the ability to relocate talents quickly are very high. It might make the difference between success and failure. Relocating an American professional to Europe is not easy. We realized this at Criteo when we wanted to bring a top talent from California to Paris. We naively thought that convincing someone from Silicon Valley to relocate would be welcomed by the French administration, which would roll out the red carpet. In fact, the red carpet was a long, rather surrealistic journey, filled with all kinds of stamps and the occasional threat to forbid the person from stepping foot on French soil, until he was finally given his resident permit. It's better to laugh than cry over it.

Going the other way is not easy either. Europeans who try to get an

American work visa know that very well. If you don't hire an expensive lawyer, it's quite hard to pull off. At Criteo, we had to fill out thousands of pages of forms and certificates. In my own case, I naively thought it would be easier. After all, I had come here to invest and create jobs for Americans. I quickly realized just how complicated the system is. The US administration demanded a complete business plan as well as copies of my engineering school diplomas and semester grades from twenty years earlier!

Does the idea of reciprocity between states push Europeans to make things very difficult for Americans who are open to relocating to the old continent? It's not very smart because unfortunately, they aren't playing on equal terms. Every high-end geek in the world wants to go to the Silicon Valley. This gives the American administration the luxury of being bureaucratic without discouraging vocations. Europe isn't an obvious destination for those who want to have a career in technology. It might be time to put diplomatic ego aside and welcome talented individuals who want to move to Europe. The old continent's young and still-fragile tech ecosystem has a great need for it.

Those Evil Labor Regulations

Now let's consider European labor regulations. Are they really the root cause of all European start-up problems? It's true that firing someone in France or Germany requires a formal process that isn't always suited to the context of start-ups. And it often costs a lot more than in the States. Social security contributions are also considerably higher. But in a certain way, these elements are already factored into the labor market. Overall in the tech sector, salaries are much lower in Paris or Berlin than in Silicon Valley or New York. Criteo provides a good example of this. When we started to grow overseas from Paris, I was often asked why we didn't fully move our research and development to the West Coast. The answer is simple: we decided to remain in Paris out of pure pragmatism. It costs us much less and gives us a competitive advantage compared to players who are relying solely on the sometimes-exorbitant compensations you see in Silicon Valley. It just goes to show that old Europe isn't doomed to systematically lose jobs. Globalization is also an opportunity to make use of comparative advantages in technology start-ups. In particular, countries that favor science and mathematics in education have a great hand to play in the future.

What about French Laziness?

The French are incredibly lazy, aren't they? It's the country that works in stops and starts in May and comes to a grinding halt in August, and so on. In France, there is a surprising pride in what we call "status", which is very different from the Anglo-Saxon approach, where professional relationships are first and foremost contractual. This particular status mindset can create a sometimes-tense social climate that leads the French to stubbornly cling to untenable principles. But with the right dynamics, it can also create a powerful professional awareness, which sometimes reaches an extremist attitude. Whether feverish or coughing, the French worker makes it a point of honor to go to work, even if it means contaminating his coworkers! It's out of the question for him to go to a doctor's appointment on work time. And when public transportation strikes come along (which unfortunately is a sticky local tradition), some people are ready to walk several hours to reach their office.

In the United States, I discovered a different system of days off that includes medical checkups, car problems, plumber appointments, snow days, and other little vagaries of daily life that have no equivalent in France. In the end, the productivity of a motivated employee is absolutely comparable in Europe and the United States. And between you and me, no matter the country, if you're dealing with an unmotivated employee, it's hard to get anything out of the person.

In 2009, my investor Dom Vidal introduced me to Jonathan Wolf, a brilliant British manager who also had cut his teeth at Yahoo! Jonathan had the daring and the foresight to join us at a time when all Criteo employees were French. When he arrived, he quickly forced us to make English the company's official language. This linguistic switch was an important element in Criteo's rapid international expansion. Aware of all the clichés about the French from his fellow Brits, Jonathan wrote a delightful blog entry on LinkedIn titled "Why You Should Hire a French Person." He starts by saying, "Yes, you read that right. And yes, I am English. So how could I say something so crazy, you ask?" And Jonathan goes on to boast of the analytic abilities of the French, due to a more systematic education in mathematics. Jonathan also insists on the creativity of French workers, which he thinks is paradoxically linked to their skeptical culture. Jonathan's blog post was widely shared on social networks, and interestingly, the people who most strongly disagreed with Jonathan's analysis were the French, of course!

How to Break the Glass Ceiling?

Highly motivated entrepreneurs are everywhere. Just consider the millions of small businesses created in the world every year. Unfortunately, this is often not enough to boost economic growth. Why not?

Is it due to the death rate of new companies? It's a fact that half of all new businesses don't survive five years. We could try to diminish these failures, but is that really the right approach? Failure is an inherent part of creation. After all, if half of the businesses created become profitable, that's already great. In the world of start-ups, the mortality rate is much higher, and this doesn't shock anyone.

The real problem lies elsewhere. In fact, among new businesses that survive infancy, there are very few that go beyond fifty or even ten employees. And that's a much bigger issue. When they survive, most small businesses remain small indefinitely, condemned to bang their heads against a sort of glass ceiling that prevents them from growing.

In Silicon Valley, there are also a tremendous number of small businesses and bankruptcies. But new rising stars emerge regularly. Some manage to become very big companies in just a decade. Rarely does this happen elsewhere. No other ecosystem in the world has been capable of creating such a density of tech giants such as Oracle, Apple, and Google.

It is interesting to note that the word "start-up" comes from the West Coast. But why use this new word? Isn't distinguishing a start-up from a small business just a matter of style, using a word that sounds cooler? We tend to translate start-up to mean "young growth company." In other words, what distinguishes a start-up from a traditional small business is most of all youth (it's a well-known fact that old people have stopped growing) and its growth rate. The result is that above a certain size, you are no longer considered a start-up. It's a statement (almost a criticism) that I hear more and more about Criteo: "Now that you are so big, you're no longer a start-up, are you?"

A start-up is not always a growth company. Some start-ups never get off the ground—the majority of them in fact. A start-up is a company *built to grow*. That may seem like a minor difference, but it has deep impacts on the structuring of almost everything that matters in building a venture.

So why are there so many small businesses and so few start-ups? In many cities in the developed world, there are all the ingredients for success: excellent schools and universities, cutting-edge infrastructure, dense industrial fabric, and abundant wealth. So why is it so hard? Why are the Apples and Googles not more evenly distributed in the developed world? They are not even evenly distributed in the United States, but rather are highly concentrated in the Silicon Valley. Those who point the blame at the tax system, the complex bureaucracy, the labor laws, and so on are fighting the wrong battle (something the French are very good at). What's missing is a little indefinable something. "It's the economy, stupid" was Bill Clinton's well-known adage. I would change that to "It's the culture, stupid."

When Companies Will Revolutionize

7

Where We Discover That Sometimes Corporations Are Behind the Times

> That night dispelled forever the long and painful dream of the thousand years of the Middle Ages. The approaching dawn was that of liberty! Since that marvelous night, no more classes, but Frenchmen; no more provinces, but one France!

When I was a boy, I spent summer at my grandfather's country house in the middle of France. This was long before iPads. There wasn't much to do, so I spent a lot of time in the old family library. Encouraged by my mother, I always had a love for books, especially history books (I try my best to instill this appreciation of history in my daughters, but with limited success, I have to admit). And this is how I discovered, in my grandfather's dusty collection, the preceding lyrical quotation from an old-school historian. This quote recalls the night of August 4, 1789, which is famous in France's mythology. That night, the French National Assembly voted to abolish feudal rights and privileges. As young Americans are raised on the saga of the Founding Fathers, France is also marked by the values of its own revolution: the abolishment of privileges and the seeking of liberty and equality.

Over time, in all developed countries, institutions evolve toward a system that is still imperfect but more inclusive. As a matter of fact, many scholars claim that inclusive institutions are the basis of a country's long-term economic prosperity. However, when it comes to the business world, you quickly realize that there the message of the aforementioned quotation is much more of a rhetoric formula than reality. So how is it that corporations—which are often eager to criticize the inefficiencies of the political world—aren't as far along in this inclusive trend as the democracies that contain them?

The Traditional Corporation, a Feudal Model

If we take a closer look, we see that most small businesses operate much like the feudal monarchies of long ago. The boss? He is the sole master on board, with almost God-given power. He sometimes founds dynasties, bequeathing his empire to his son or daughter. The king is dead; long live the king! Of course, there are all kinds of monarchs, from the fatherly boss to an enlightened despot, such as Frederick the Great, or an absolute autocrat such as Louis XIV. It's a little subtler in large corporations where there is a slightly more delicate balance of power between executives, employees, and shareholders.

It should be said that the old autocratic model—seen as the alpha and omega by the majority of business owners—can very well work for companies in traditional sectors. You have a boss who sets the rules, and everything follows suit accordingly. All employees have a precise role that they must respect. But when instead of indefinitely reproducing the same thing, you need creativity, inventiveness, and innovation, this whole autocratic model breaks down.

The pace of change introduced by digital technologies has no equivalent in prior technological revolutions. I'm not talking about incremental innovation (which consists of doing a little bit better than what we already do), but *disruptive* innovation (which consists of killing what we have previously done and starting over from zero). Disruptive innovation is the raison d'être of most start-ups. Each start-up is aiming in its own way to find the new concept that will disrupt the established order.

The HBO series *Silicon Valley* describes this phenomenon with school-kid humor. In one episode, we see a bunch of start-ups take the stage to pitch their big ideas to a jury of experts. Each presentation grandiloquently concludes with "We want to *change the world*." You might say that these geeks indeed have some delusions of grandeur. And you laugh. But actually, what's even funnier is that this is how it actually works in real life. All start-ups *really* want to change the world. Otherwise, they don't have the right DNA to succeed.

Unfortunately, creativity can't be ordered. Inventing a technology that works is hard. Scaling this technology into a global leader is another challenge altogether. In the tech sector, the typical five-year plan doesn't work.

Silicon Valley and the Invention of Inclusive Corporations

Silicon Valley has something unique about it. I won't mention its scientific universities, which can be found elsewhere, or the proximity to money, which is abundant in many big cities, or its very pleasant climate (though this is a definite advantage!). No, the real power of the Bay Area is something else. The Valley has an inclusive culture that is unique in the business world. It's the polar opposite of the autocratic culture that dominates the traditional world of small businesses. And this inclusive culture is what gave birth to the whole idea of tech start-ups.

Some say this has to do with the conquest of the American frontier. At the time, crossing the United States was a long and dangerous journey. The pioneers had to face numerous unexpected situations and adapt as best as they could. Those who managed to cross all the way to the Pacific needed to be remarkably adaptable. One of the keys to survival was forming alliances with other pioneers to create wagon trains that followed the same route together. Uniting with perfect strangers? There is nothing more contradictory to common sense. Why trust strangers who might slit your throat at the first opportunity? And yet this trust, this recognition that we are stronger together than separately, this idea of sharing complementary skills to pursue an ambitious goal, this is exactly the start-up spirit. What makes this specific culture so extraordinary? It completely breaks from the overwhelming majority of human cultures the world has known since the dawn of time.

Coworking, Flat-Sharing, Ride-Sharing—Sharing Is Everywhere

Sharing is in the air. Very fashionable are coworking spaces, which are shared office spaces where numerous entrepreneurs and projects mingle together. Each team works independently, but this mix creates a spirit that benefits everyone (and sometimes changes destinies, such as when I met Franck and Romain). Soaring housing prices? Flat-sharing and temporary accommodations are thriving. It's enough to make the traditional hotel industry panic.

Sharing is the rediscovery of a powerful concept. At one moment or another in your life, you have to face issues (often financial ones) that your close friends and family can't help you with. The solution is to turn to strangers and trust them. If their interests are—at least temporarily—aligned with yours, there is a good chance that these strangers will behave in a good way.

The Internet has allowed this sharing culture to grow to a level unimaginable in the traditional economy. Just consider how infrequently hitchhiking was used (and with very limited success, I can guarantee you). In some countries, the Internet has turned ride-sharing into a veritable industry that has created serious competition for trains (not in the United States, where there are virtually no trains). Similarly, the sharing economy is also very present in how digital technology itself is built, such as the fascinating movement around open-source software. Criteo itself relies heavily on many open technologies.

Silicon Valley–Style Sharing

When my wife and I started our organic soup and salad stand, we were stunned to discover the traditional world of small businesses. It was quite far from the idyllic image we had. It was a world filled with suspicion, jealousy, and individualism, in which neighbors glared at each other. Every shopkeeper had little tricks he had garnered over time. But there was no way he would share his experience with others. I saw how a lemon balsamic dressing could become a more closely guarded secret than the plans for the atomic bomb. It was also impossible to get the phone number to a reliable fruit and vegetable supplier. Each newcomer was forced to make all the mistakes his predecessors had made as they watched on with glee. There's no reason it should be easier for rookies than for old hands, right?

In comparison, the world of the Internet is the polar opposite of this. Of course there is fierce competition. Many are called, but few are chosen. But there is also a shared sense that we aren't in a zero-sum game in which some succeed at the expense of others. It's in everyone's interest that some of us succeed. Each success reinforces the overall ecosystem, which indirectly benefits everyone. Call it the sharing spirit.

Expand Your Personal Network

The first thing I would advise a young entrepreneur to do is exchange ideas with his or her peers. This great thing about the Internet sector is that no matter your origins, studies, or family, there is a way in. You don't have to have graduated from an Ivy League college to join the dance. What a breath of fresh air this is compared to a lot of traditional sectors where if you are not from the inner circle, you won't be accepted.

People often agree to meet a young college dropout who appears out of nowhere with an interesting story—because everyone is keenly aware that this young person might be the next Mark Zuckerberg. Who could have imagined ten years ago that Facebook, a site that started off as a student-ranking site, would become the social passport for a large part of humanity? That Twitter and its tweets would be a major medium of the Arab Spring? Technological revolutions always appear in an unlikely manner. Despising the youth is not only an arrogant attitude of those who have succeeded; it's a real mistake for those who want to understand the future. Bill Gates's real fear wasn't the ferocious competition he had with other big tech players, those gorillas rolling in cash. No, he had nightmares about some kid in a garage inventing something that one day would undermine his entire empire.

When I moved to Silicon Valley, I visited some local gurus. The goal wasn't to find the solution to my immediate problems. Sometimes the conversations weren't even very interesting. But sometimes, a seemingly insignificant sentence made me suddenly put together obscure pieces in my mind, like having a burst of intuition. For example, I spoke to many former Yahoo! executives who explained to me how this old net star had been crushed by Google. What came up repeatedly was the lack of technology investment, especially when the portal was at the height of its glory. I could sense their frustration about this missed opportunity. Thanks to these conversations, I became obsessed with the idea of making research and development an absolute priority at Criteo. In hindsight, this is exactly what allowed us to stay ahead of the game when along with our success came the inevitable army of clones trying to copy our product.

I didn't become a guru myself. But now, because of Criteo's visibility, many entrepreneurs come to me with questions about how to scale their own business. Why do I take those meetings? Still the same idea: I'm giving back what was given to me, not to those who gave to me, but to others, who will then give on to others still.

The nature of Silicon Valley is to integrate newcomers very quickly. High-end immigration is the highest in the world. A large fraction of new local start-ups have founders who were born outside the United States. No other place in the world is like that.

The Culture of Trust

For Criteo, I tried to express this idea of inclusiveness in a short manifesto posted on our corporate website:

> I've joined Criteo, a global team of people who share a common belief in the culture of collaborative innovation and entrepreneurship.
> I'm open to learning from others and I will also help nurture learning in others.
> I agree to pay forward whatever positive benefits I receive from anyone. In particular, for every hour of help I receive, I will give an hour of help to someone else. For every risk someone takes for me, I will take risk with a different person.
> We will bring people together, as none of us is as smart as all of us. We understand that mistakes are acceptable ways of testing new ideas and improving each of us.
> We will treat everyone fairly.
> Every day, each of us will act as a role model for the company.
> We will dream, lead, experiment, iterate and persist to create superior and sustainable value for our clients.

Okay, I admit that sounds a little over the top. Way back when I was a foot soldier lost in a large corporation, I would have greeted this manifesto with a good dose of (French) irony. Perhaps my American experience and the experience of leading a global business have changed my perspective. When you have more than 1,500 employees spread around the world, it's important to reaffirm common values. I often hear people make fun of Google's "Don't be evil" slogan. But I guess that it represents a much stronger bond than we can imagine in a corporation that has become gigantic.

The sharing culture makes an important assumption: you have to trust in advance and not after the fact. This doesn't come intuitively. Everyone knows the story of the fox in *The Little Prince*, who requires an incredible amount of time and patience to be tamed. This is undeniably a beautiful, poetic idea. Isn't the feeling of friendship one of the most powerful human feelings that exists? But in the business world, this kind of cautious behavior is an enormous restraint. If it takes you ten years to step out of your ivory tower to talk to a potential business partner or let a financial investor come close, you will never be able to build much of anything. Today everything goes too fast.

Unlike the usual give-give dynamic, you also have to be willing to give without necessarily receiving anything back. It's the same logic as in a peer-to-peer program. You certainly aren't forced to share, but if everyone decides not to give anything to the community, it won't work. Of course, some people don't play the game. There are those who don't return the favor, who take without ever giving. In game theory, this is called a "free rider." Reputations are made quickly. Free riders get spotted, as if the sharing ecosystem generates antibodies to protect its culture.

One particular kind of free rider is one who has become specialized in the questionable field of professional connecting. So many newcomers show up in the Valley that this has become a real business. Professional connectors promise you the moon; they promise that they will introduce you to everyone who matters, that they will give you a ticket to the inner circles. Of course, for the newcomer who doesn't know anyone, the idea of having another person build a network for you is rather attractive. In exchange for their amazing relationship-building services, these network consultants charge high fees. Avoid them. Most of the time, their added value is paltry. But more importantly, their behavior is completely contrary to the Silicon Valley spirit. Here, you don't make a profit by just connecting people; you have to bring something else to the table.

How to Build the Founding Team

8

Why a Solitary Entrepreneur Is Likely Headed for Failure

Three founders is the Criteo model. Is it reasonable to turn a single example into a general rule? After all, why bother setting off on this adventure with someone else? It seems easier to imagine oneself as "master of the universe."

And yet statistics are merciless. Start-ups built by one single founder take an average of seventy-two months to become profitable. This drops to thirty-six months as soon as you add a second cofounder. Even more striking, in the past fifteen years, 80 percent of tech start-ups that have reached the symbolic one-billion-dollar valuation (the so-called unicorns) have had at least two founders. That is also the case of most home runs such as Google, Microsoft, and Apple. Everyone knows the names Bill Gates for Microsoft and Steve Jobs for Apple. Not many people know the names of their cofounders. But that doesn't mean that it was a one-man show behind the scenes. On the contrary, in these examples, each cofounder brought something unique to the mix that has proven to be a key element in the success. There are counterexamples, of course, such as Dell. But creating a tech giant remains incredibly difficult. For ordinary mortals (which I am acutely aware of being), maximizing chances for success requires cofounders.

Asking Family, Friends, or Strangers?

Though I was completely unaware of the aforementioned statistics, I always wanted to build companies with other people. I just felt like sharing this powerful experience with people close to me. But finding friends who wanted to do this at the same time I did wasn't easy. They weren't all necessarily obsessed with the idea of creating a start-up as I was. However, at the beginning, I never would have imagined jumping into this adventure with total strangers the way I ended up doing with Franck and Romain after our unexpected encounter in the incubator.

How do you choose your cofounders? For a small-business owner, the first move is to turn to your family. What could be more natural? Business has a reputation of being ruthless. In this hostile world, it would seem reasonable to join forces with people whom you trust the most. Actually, the family model works well in the case of traditional skills that are handed down, transmitted from parent to offspring. In the digital world, you don't have time to transmit anything from one generation to the next. Things simply move too fast. The tech world is complex and unpredictable. It's rare to have a sibling, a child, or a cousin who is exactly complementary to you. By favoring personal connections, you risk lacking some critical skills required to make your project successful, not to mention the emotional factor that can particularly complicate daily life. Consider Microsoft, Apple, and Google again. None of these titans was founded by a family but were started by duos of professionals.

Looking across Europe, it's interesting to see how this family culture influences business ventures. There is a rather clear-cut distinction between what we could call a Latin model and the Nordic model. For the Latin model, Italy has the most developed culture of *la famiglia*. Family-owned small and medium-size businesses are the foundation of the Italian economy, especially in luxury goods and the clothing industry. But this model did not adapt very well to the digital economy. Today, Yoox is one of the rare Italian Internet start-ups to have scaled globally, and its organization is more similar to Silicon Valley models than to a traditional Italian small business. The same shortcomings exist in Spain, where one struggles to name a world-class digital leader. On the other hand, Sweden has produced an extraordinary number of highly successful start-ups that have expanded globally. Skype and Spotify are undoubtedly the most visible, but there are many others. It's not by chance. This small country already has a very robust, inclusive culture. It was natural for the Swedish to absorb Silicon Valley's special culture. And where are France and Germany in all this? They have a blend of both models—not totally Latin, not really Nordic either, often still mistrustful of people who aren't from the inner circle.

And friends? We have all been raised on the myth of the bunch of buddies who change the world in their garage. This works only if the friends in question are real professionals and not just drinking buddies. I still remember a relevant scene from the series *Silicon Valley*. The founder does a skills assessment of his team. He realizes that his best friend doesn't bring anything to the project and that his presence in the casting sticks out like a sore thumb. After a lot of thinking, he makes an incredibly difficult and yet necessary decision: to remove him from the project. Though he often looks like a foolish teenager, in this scene the founder hero of the series demonstrates surprising maturity and lucidity.

The Limits of Friends and Family

A typical novice entrepreneur, I was molded by my birth culture. For Kallback, my first company, I built my capitalization table with the people I trusted most: my brother, my father, and a few very close friends. As I said previously, it was a total fiasco (not their fault, but mine). For Kiwee, my second company, I gave my friends just minor stakes. This allowed me to keep a large part of the capital to recruit full-time cofounders. Finally, for Criteo, I went one step further, to the point that my father and brother, who had invested in my first fiasco, joked a lot that they had been invited only for the bankruptcy, not for the jackpot. It's somewhat true.

Nevertheless, I had learned that doing a "friends and family" pre-seed round results in a mix of styles that isn't easy to handle. With Kallback and Kiwee, I should have treated my father and my buddies like any other business angels. But this wasn't easy. In fact, I gave them more capital than I would have given a regular outside investor. I didn't see the problem. After all, it's rather nice to share your adventure with family and close friends. But complications arise later when you have to bring on board talented executives and professional investors—because there is just less capital available for the newcomers.

You also have to make the distinction between the real founders of a start-up and those who just accompany them. It's like the old joke of how to make bacon and eggs. The hen is involved in the project, but the pig is committed body and soul. It's the same for founders. Yes, maybe you have talked extensively about your project with your friend Ben. Perhaps he even dedicated two or three weekends as your sparring partner, producing some valuable fresh ideas. That's not the point. If Ben continues to work in his bank while you have dropped everything for your start-up, your friend can't claim to be a founder. His access to capital should remain very limited, and he will have to settle for the title of business angel, mentor, or adviser. There is nothing dishonorable in that. It's just the way it is, and to avoid any misunderstanding, it's better to clarify these things with him right from the start.

Quite often, I encounter start-ups where this issue is a bit muddy. For example, there was an entrepreneur who was pitching me his new mobile app, which sounded promising. When I asked him what his role in the team was, he explained that he was still working full-time in his old company and that he was participating in the project at night and on weekends. After I dug further, he admitted that 75 percent of the capital was held by three pseudo-founders who contributed to the project only on Sundays. The remaining meager 25 percent was left to the only two actual cofounders who were really working full-time. This kind of setup makes any serious investor run away as fast as his legs can carry him.

Over the years, I had to overcome my own mental barriers. With time, I came to better understand what's so special about tech start-ups, which helped me that day in the incubator in Paris when I impulsively decided to bind my fate to Franck and Romain. They were total strangers but had exactly the skills I needed. It changed everything.

The Magic of Stock Options

9

Stock Options or Nothing

Whether a company should share equity with employees is not obvious to everyone. I can still picture a dinner in a fancy restaurant with a bunch of business owners of all kinds, back when I was in Europe. At one point, I casually asked the audience, "So who here gives stock options to his employees?" I glanced around with delight, well aware that it was a touchy topic.

After some hesitation, the answers were mostly negative: "I prefer giving them a good cash bonus." "We don't expect to go public, so it's not relevant for us." "It's not something my employees request."

I did have two pioneers in front of me, though: "I give stock options to my direct reports." "It's a tool that I save for the executive committee and some rare talents."

"Only the top of the pyramid?" I asked. "What about the other employees?"

The answer came roaring back: "For other employees, it would be like throwing pearls before swine. I mean, it would be a waste because most of the time they don't understand how it works."

Pearls before swine—that said it all.

For most business owners outside the Valley, the idea of attributing stock options to everyone seems incongruous. And strangely, no one seems to complain about it, not even the workers, as if they think it is a losing battle. I remember that some of my first employees in France, when hired, were more interested in lunch vouchers than in stock options. Of course, this was before Criteo became the success that it did.

Why? It's the eternal division between labor and capital—so eternal that it seems immutable. For many business owners, questioning it seems futile. I admit that it also took me a while to understand it. In Europe, even pure Internet start-ups don't all give stock options to their employees. A lot of them distribute them at best in micro doses to a minimum of people.

Relocating to the West Coast completely changed my perspective. I remember interviewing my office manager in Palo Alto. It was my first hire after Margo, and I was still a complete barbarian in Silicon Valley. At the end of the hiring interview, I asked the usual question: "Are there any topics we didn't discuss that you would like to bring up?"

"Yes. I'd like to know how many stock options are planned for this position," she asked me in the most natural way.

I suddenly realized that in Silicon Valley it was unimaginable to join a start-up without being offered stock options, even for a position that required rather standard qualifications. "Stock options" was the magic term here, the foundation of the social compact. More than a simple financial carrot, it was rather a ticket to a dream. We all go on an adventure together, and maybe, at the end of the trip, we will reach the pirates' treasure island.

I answered her quickly. "Um, yes, of course. I don't know the exact amount, but I'll get back to you about it right away."

At that point, I decided to give stock options to everyone at Criteo, in every country. When I see the dynamic that this created over time, I have to say that I don't regret my decision.

The Criteo Millionaires

At the time of the IPO, Criteo has created fifty millionaires among our employees, and this number continues to grow with each quarter. Among them are some amazing stories, such as the iconoclast who joined us as a part-time intern just because he spoke Italian, or the friendly guitarist who knew nothing about the Internet. Combining extraordinary pugnacity and uncommon smartness, the latter employee grew up with Criteo to eventually lead an international team of fifty professionals.

I remember a software developer who was as discreet as she was efficient. She came with me from Kiwee, where she hadn't earned very much. She joined the Criteo team first in Paris, then in Palo Alto, and finally in New York. She earned more money than she could have imagined at the start of the adventure, and it was more than well deserved. I'm truly happy for her.

One of the most amazing paths is undoubtedly that of Pascal, who joined Criteo as our marketing and sales director at the time we were discovering advertising. He then become our COO before leaving us one year before the IPO. He had an exceptional flair for business but was a college dropout. In a more traditional sector, it would have been very hard to imagine this type of stellar career, especially in France, where academic diplomas are so stupidly important.

I love these amazing individual stories. I am also very proud to see all these new start-ups created by former Criteo employees or people directly inspired by our story. I hope there will be more, many more. It's rather nice to hear young entrepreneurs claiming that they want to become "the Criteo of this" or "the Criteo of that."

There are a lot of talks about the breakdown of the social ladder. I like the idea that technology has the power to reshuffle the cards, that there's no old elite capable of protecting its privileges against new entrants.

How to Pay in a Start-Up

Like mushrooms in the forest, controversies about CEO compensation pop up in the press on a regular basis—sometimes a spicy scandal to gobble up, a massive golden parachute that dominates the headlines, a huge bonus that arrives right when the company has announced sweeping layoffs.

I wasn't very interested in executive compensation for a long time. I was mostly focused on the growth of my start-up, and everything else seemed secondary. In fact, at the start of Kiwee and Criteo, I had no salary at all. That's the fate of every founder. When I started Kiwee, I had enough savings to live for a year without external resources. It wasn't much, but at that time I had neither a family nor a mortgage. For Criteo, I had a financial cushion from the sale of Kiwee. Founders without a salary generally last until the series A. After the first investment round with the VC comes the question of founders' compensation. Basic good governance says the investors should decide the founders' salary. When founders and VCs have the right state of mind around the table, this discussion is easy. Most of a founder's financial upside isn't made through his salary but hopefully through future capital gains. So the general practice is to pay founders enough to allow them to maintain their lifestyle without excessive stress. So no big salary, not even a market-level salary, but still a decent salary. As an investor, the last thing you want is a founder whose professional bandwidth is contaminated by personal financial issues.

And then every year, the situation is reevaluated according to the same criteria. For Criteo, I had a sort of annual interview, almost like a regular employee. During this discussion, I either asked for a raise or did not, making sure my request was reasonable enough to cut short any unnecessary discussion with my investors. When revenues started to take off, we had a little more leeway. But to remain in the start-up spirit, we always stayed far below what I could have claimed as market price for my profile. It was also out of the question to supplement my income with yearly dividends. The whole idea of dividends is almost foreign to the world of high-growth tech start-ups. Even when Criteo became profitable, our cash surplus was always carefully kept in-house to fund our future growth.

This way of handling my salary lasted for the first eight years of the company's life. In early 2013, when we started to get ready to go public, things changed. We had to ask ourselves many new questions linked to the fact that my compensation was about to enter the public domain. In other words, we were going to have to justify my pay in the eyes of the world. For this, the easiest route was to look at market practices for similarly sized public companies. By taking the average of twenty publicly listed tech start-ups, we came up with a solid benchmark of market practices. And here we were surprised to discover that I was paid far less than my colleagues. Through magic or the pernicious effect of benchmarking, the board of directors decided to give me a very significant raise to shift me right to the middle of the sample pack. Generally speaking, we try to pay our employees neither too much nor too little compared to the rest of the ad tech sector. In principle, this practice of matching the market avoids aberrations. But at the same time, in a bull market for talents, this system tends to create inflationary mechanisms that are hard to control for companies that previously have practiced moderation.

Every year, we begin this calibration all over again. As you can imagine, compensation of named officers is correlated to the company's size. Since Criteo grew quickly, we were always comparing ourselves to bigger and bigger companies. How do you know whether the CEO's compensation is at the right level? Was I really smarter than a boss who struggles with a company in a distressed sector such as steel or manufacturing? It's hard to say. The fact remains that this touchy question of CEO salaries creates great opportunities for consultants who specialize in compensation studies. They write lovely reports loaded with statistics, comparisons, and recommendations on good practices. This approach has the merit of giving a scientific veneer to an easily flammable topic; it is a way of defusing any eventual controversy by making the question of salaries something defined by the market outside the company.

For the past several years, executive compensation has tended to increase faster than inflation—and faster than the average employee salary. It's a fact proven by figures. Still, it's normal to pay a top executive well because his or her impact is usually critical to the business. Great, mediocre, and bad executive decisions make a big difference on a company's trajectory. The ability to make these stressful decisions should be well compensated. But with how much exactly? In large organizations, situations are inherently complex, usually with many people involved. It is hard to distinguish exactly what each party specifically merits. For a board of directors, which by definition has only limited awareness of day-to-day operations, it's even more complicated.

It's impossible to put an absolute dollar value on someone. In many sectors, those closest to the money—the financiers, the salespeople— tend to take the lion's share. But it's different in the world of start-ups. Technology is the heart of the system and is what dictates the pace of the company. At Criteo, we pay particular attention to developers. The very people who are still treated as second-class citizens in most traditional companies are our stars. Call it the revenge of the geeks.

What about the Luck Factor in Personal Success?

From the first industrial revolution, every generation has had its adventures around new emerging sectors—oil and steel at the end of the nineteenth century, the automobile at the beginning of the twentieth century. Today we are experiencing an even more amazing revolution. Digital technology is progressing at a much faster pace than past upheavals. I feel lucky to be living in such extraordinary times. That said, to really benefit from it, you still must enter the sector at the right time of your life.

I recall a dinner at the end of 1999 with a former colleague from Lucent, the telecom manufacturer where I began my career. We were sitting in front of plates of pasta carbonara and having a lively conversation.

"Well, I just started fundraising for Kiwee. It's so exciting. What about you? Didn't you tell me you were going to create a start-up one day? When are you going to do it?"

"It's easy for you. You're not married, you don't have kids, and you don't have a mortgage. I can't live without a salary. I should have leapt in seven years ago, when I didn't have any of the constraints I do now. But just remember that back then, no one was talking about the Internet yet. The problem is our sector, telecoms. Once you get in, it's hard to get out."

At that instant I realized that I had almost missed the bus too. Among the skills I had wanted to master during my academic years, English was very high on the list. So for my last year in college, I had insisted on going to London. To get there, I had to choose a telecommunication major, quite far from my love for computer programming. But back then, it seemed like a simple detour from my initial plan. In the 1990s, this sector seemed to have huge potential—but not for everyone. My telecom major insidiously pushed me in the wrong direction. At the time, the really attractive telecom start-ups were mobile operators that were flourishing in every country with spectacular growth. But to build a mobile operator, you had to get not only an expensive license; you also needed an investment capacity that was far beyond the reach of the junior naive entrepreneur I was. My first attempt at entrepreneurship would then be the least attractive fringe of the sector, call-back services. A not-so-great product combined with amateur execution sent me into bankruptcy in less than six months.

Eating his pasta, my friend started laughing and said, "And your new gig in ringtones, Kiwee, it's still highly telco dependent, right? I hope it doesn't bring you bad luck. Here, I propose a toast to all losers stuck in the telecom sector, while the real fun is in Internet software!"

We clinked glasses. My friend didn't talk much about it, but I sensed he wasn't having too much fun in his job. That was easy to understand. I had lasted only a few years in the world of traditional corporations. With Kiwee, I had remained in the hard-to-disrupt telecom sector. Okay, it was supposed to be mobile Internet, but back in the pre-iPhone days, mobile Internet was just a cool concept with very little substance to it. The technology was in its infancy, and the user experience was really poor. To top it all off, brainless mobile operators had the power of life and death over small content providers like me—thus, Kiwee's mitigated success. And yet this experience was decisive. It helped me finally understand better how the start-up ecosystem worked. I gained enough self-confidence to start Criteo, and the rest is history. Nevertheless, it was a close call. One step too far in the wrong direction, and I might have been stuck for good in the entrepreneur dead zone.

My friend sighed as he put down his glass, as if he had heard my thoughts. He concluded: "Professional career is a real game of chance. You have to be born at the right time, neither too young nor too old. And of course, you can't afford to miss the most promising sector of your time."

So my message for young ambitious entrepreneurs who want to create their own start-ups is not to wait. The world of digital technology moves very fast. There's no need to mope for years in a big corporation to acquire some experience. Tomorrow's young geek will be the next star whose face will dominate a giant screen in Times Square.

Only the Stars Survive | 10

Go Big or Go Home

Maybe you remember Nike's rather brutal slogan "You don't win silver, you lose gold." This is confirmed in various Olympic photos in which the gold medalist is beaming at the top of the podium while the silver medalist can't help but scowl. Sometimes the difference was a mere tenth of a second. But that's too bad. The unfortunate silver medalist knows that the media and posterity will remember only the winner. An even more explicit formulation of this idea is the saying "Second place is the first loser." Is that clear enough?

In the tech world, an oft-quoted adage is "Winner takes all." Look at Google. In just a few years, it completely killed almost all competition in the search business. Facebook? It wiped the first generation of social networks off the map. As for Uber, the only thing slowing its company from overwhelming the private urban transport sector is local legislation protecting taxis.

In this globalized world, the rewards are so enormous for the leader that you have to give yourself every chance to succeed. Go big or go home. In other words, if you feel you have a slight advantage, you have to charge forward like tomorrow is the last day of your life. For a start-up, this means that if you are focusing only on some local market, sooner rather than later, you will be marginalized. There is no other choice but to aim at world domination. Right from the start, you have to conceive your product so that it can go global. Each small detail matters, including the choice of a name. What about Criteo's name? According to the legend, Criteo means "I predict" in ancient Greek, which is a cool reference to our core expertise. But most of all, Criteo is short, easy to remember, and sufficiently generic to use for any product (which is very useful when you pivot three times, as we did).

This is also why we accepted so much capital dilution during the private life of Criteo. Without all this money, nothing would have been possible. It gave us the means to persist until we could find the winning formula. We approached each new step with the same mind-set. When we had to finance our expansion in the United States, we invested nearly $20 million before this market became profitable. At that time, it was a huge burden on our cash. But if you hope to win the gold medal in any tech category, it's impossible to overlook the US market. Without America, Criteo would have been doomed to play in the minor leagues.

Things haven't always been that way. In the Old World, second-place companies could often do very well. In fragmented multilocal markets, there was a way to carve out a comfortable niche. But in a globalized transparent market, this isn't possible anymore. Why would clients choose the number two if they can have access to the number one? And if there is a sector where it is particularly easy for clients to access the number one, it's digital advertising technology. Since Criteo has gone public, it has grown much faster than our small local competitors. In our way, we are a good illustration of this winner-takes-all dynamic.

When Goliath Finds Himself Powerless against David

Still, winner-takes-all does not necessary last forever. Often the one thing that can make a dominant player wobble is another round of disruptive innovation. Eight-hundred-pound gorillas can fall quickly from their dominant position, sometimes in just a few years. When a tornado such as Airbnb emerges, not only does it put pressure on the traditional offline players in the tourism sector, but it's also a challenge to the first generation of Internet travel portals.

Yesterday's masters on the decline are often accused of being dinosaurs unable to evolve or adapt to what's new. Goliath is not stupid. He just discovers with dread that David is using an unexpected weapon against which he has no good response. I occasionally meet executives who are battling against disruptive competitors. Deep down, they understand very clearly what is going on. But what to do when this newcomer undermines the very foundations of your business? Unfortunately, most often there isn't any good solution. Embracing the change, assuming it's technically and culturally feasible, would mean destroying the entire business model. No company wants to dig its own grave. The most pragmatic approach often is to keep squeezing the very last dollars out of the old model until the end. The agony can last for years. Admittedly, this kind of slow death isn't exactly exciting for the teams managing the fortress under siege. Their mission is to keep the lights on for as long as possible before closing shop. To make things even worse, you can be sure that the company's best talents have already jumped ship—painful but a typical by-product of creative destruction.

There are multiple examples of waves of technology washing away the former stars. One of the most telling is the story of Yahoo!, the general-interest portal that dominated the Internet until the early 2000s. It wasn't dethroned by another general-interest portal offering a better service. It was overtaken by a radical innovation, a web page providing nothing but a simple search engine box: Google. One day a new start-up might come and disrupt Criteo. If that does happen, there is little chance it will be a Criteo clone that just reproduces what we do. It will very likely be a radical innovation that will be hard for us to react against.

In the 1990s, you had to put a lot of money on the table to build a web platform. Computer servers were expensive and not very powerful, and technologies were difficult to deploy on a large scale. Fifteen years later, things have changed considerably. In particular, the mobile app revolution has created an incredible frictionless way to distribute smart software to the masses. It's fascinating to see very small teams launch an app that is adopted in no time by millions of fans.

For instance, the gaming industry has always been a hit business, where a small fraction of the games reap most of the profits. But with the emergence of the app store model, this winner-takes-all pattern has reached a whole new dimension. An extreme case is Supercell, the Finnish game studio that developed *Clash of Clans*. Created in 2010, this start-up was acquired three years later for $1.5 billion. At the time of the deal, the company had a mere hundred employees. All its amazing growth had required remarkably little capital. I like this sector a lot because even if the chances of achieving global success are statistically slim, the entry ticket is also very reasonable. For the right creative teams, it's a pretty fascinating playing field. There is just so much more to invent in gaming without risking exhaustion, and I could see myself personally investing in this area in the future.

The Star Effect among Employees

This growing concentration of value among corporations is also well known in show business and the sporting world. But in recent years, this winner-takes-all dynamic has spread to more and more jobs. Among lawyers, doctors, engineers, and financiers, a small brilliant minority is capturing an ever-growing part of the pie, while the masses are becoming more financially insecure and having a harder and harder time earning a living from their jobs. In Silicon Valley, the giant tech players have gone so far to pamper certain star employees that those golden handcuffs make it almost impossible for them to go work elsewhere. Meanwhile, others who look just as qualified on paper struggle to find a job. Those who were unlucky enough to choose the wrong sector can find themselves unemployed after years of hard work. It's unfair, but that's how it is. Among employees too, stars carry the day.

The Obsession with Taxes | 11

Money, a Function of Diminishing Returns

I am one of the winners of the system. So I am not going to bite the hand that feeds me. I'm not ashamed of having earned money. But I don't consider it a measure of self-esteem or an end in itself. Wealth provides something particularly interesting: freedom of choice. It extends the range of possibilities. All human life is limited by intrinsic physical constraints. We are all subject to gravity. We live, and we die. Financial comfort is a way of temporarily lifting yourself from this weight and feeling a little less limited.

Nevertheless, I have noticed that the effect of money follows the law of diminishing returns. What does this lovely mathematical expression mean (once an engineer, always an engineer)? When I had my first internship in a company, I earned nearly $1,000 in monthly salary. Pocket money like this seemed incredible, a real fortune. Until then, I had lived very frugally, with a student's diet of grated carrots and rice. All of a sudden, I could go to restaurants, buy a nice meal, and go to the movies without a second thought. This was a tremendous change, with an immediate and very real impact on my daily life. As I progressed in my career, I earned more and more money. This, of course, allowed me to buy more stuff, including a car and then my home.

But with each new level I reached, the amount needed to move to the next level grew. In other words, when your income goes from $1,000 to $2,000 per month, the impact on your daily life is massive. You can do so many more things with an extra $1,000. At the other extreme, if you go from $1 million to $2 million per year, it doesn't change your daily life very much, simply because you have already covered not only your basic needs but also most of your (reasonable) desires. This is why money has diminishing returns. The more you have, the less earning more has a concrete impact on your life.

Now that I am officially a multimillionaire, this question of money becomes even more abstract. Don't ask me how much exactly I have. I don't know precisely. I'm not being cheeky; because of Criteo stock's daily changes on the stock market, I can earn or lose millions of dollars in the same day. This remains virtual, and it's better not to think about it, or it can drive you crazy. I guess the real luxury is no longer worrying about how much you make and just knowing that you have enough in your bank account that you never have to look at prices when you go shopping.

The Danger of Becoming a Rich Old Schmuck

I had already earned some of this financial ease when my previous start-up, Kiwee, was acquired in 2004. I remember looking at my bank account statement after I sold Kiwee like it was yesterday. I had never seen so many zeros. This money changed my life. Other than my apartment in Paris, I was also able to buy a lovely home in the French Alps where my family lived for a while. I was basically able to buy everything a reasonably successful fifty-five-year-old executive could hope for, but at the age of thirty-five. I even calculated that if I lived in moderation, I could probably retire thirty years ahead of schedule. The feeling of having finally gotten free was psychologically dizzying. From now on, I could do anything—even become a total loser or play video games until I fried my brain (I admit that I tried this for a while, and it is terrifying to see how quickly you can become an antisocial zombie).

Suddenly, I also had the incredibly luxury of being able to try new things, without much fear of failure. When I started Criteo, I thought that I already had enough money. So the venture wasn't about making a fortune. My goal was more to see if I could do something bigger than anything I had been able to accomplish before and, who knows, change the world a little in my own way.

Of course, like everyone who hits the jackpot, my first move was to satisfy a few whims. After Kiwee, for the first time in my life, I had more money than I needed for daily life. I decided to say good-bye to used cars and buy a new one. When you think about it, buying a new car is absurd, especially for someone like me, who couldn't care less about cars.

But a whim is a whim, and I left the dealership behind the wheel of my brand-spanking-new metallic-gray car. I drove a few dozen miles to enjoy my shiny toy. It had that new-car smell and was spacious and comfortable. But there was a detail that bothered me. I couldn't get used to the panoramic sunroof that I had really insisted on when I ordered the car. It made the interior rather noisy. And the additional light mostly benefited the rear passengers, which made the option not that interesting.

The next day, I went back to visit the dealership. "Hello again. Do you remember me? I bought a car yesterday. Actually, I'd like the same one, but without the sunroof."

"Oh, I'm afraid that's impossible. We can't go back," he said to me, seeming a little put-out and like he was bracing for a long, drawn-out discussion.

"What do you mean it's impossible? Can't you just buy it back and sell me another one? You do that every day, don't you?"

"You would like to resell the car you bought yesterday?" he asked slowly, to make sure he understood.

"Yes, and right away, if possible."

"You'll have to resell it in the used car department, and it will cost you," he said cautiously. "You're going to lose $4,000 at the very least."

"I don't care."

"Okay, whatever you want," he said in astonishment. "I'll see what we have in stock."

His reaction disturbed me. I started to think about it. This outburst wasn't me. In fact, I was acting like a schmuck, a capricious and arrogant schmuck, exactly the kind of person who horrified my parents—and horrified me too. After all, this sunroof was very nice.

So I said to him a little sheepishly, "Well, actually, I'll keep it. Thanks. I'm sorry for the bother."

Welcome to the Rich World

Money doesn't provide everything. But rich people often have the illusion that money gives them knowledge. For me, having come from a rather intellectual household (in which the word "rich" often went with "old" and "ugly"), this is hard to understand. I am always stunned to see how other rich people think they know everything. It's funny that those who didn't earn their money themselves are the ones who are most confident.

As I said earlier, I lived in the French Alps with my family for a while, including during the first couple of years of Criteo. I commuted to Paris from Monday to Friday and enjoyed the fresh air of the mountains during the weekends. To pass time in the off-season, I tried my hand at golf, more out of idleness than real passion. One Sunday in early summer, as I was about to leave the posh resort's golf club, I noticed in the parking lot a clean-cut fat man in his sixties walking toward me with determination.

"Do you have a car? Would you mind dropping me off at my chalet? It's only five minutes from here," he asked.

"No problem," I said. "Get in."

He sat down next to me, and I started to drive. Like many geeks, I'm not always sociable, but sometimes you have to make an effort. In order to start a conversation, I asked, "Do you often come to Méribel on vacation?"

"I bought my chalet ten years ago, but I don't know if I'll stay here. The wealth tax has become unbearable. I pay literally a fortune. I can't take it anymore. And the government only thinks of adding on. They don't understand anything. At this pace, we're all going to end up penniless. The country is ruined, and all they think of is taxing us more."

I had let this stranger into my car, and instead of having a friendly conversation about the weather, the snow, the mountains, he was moaning about his money. I could see he wasn't about to stop. The tirade continued in a predictable way about the good-for-nothings, the idlers, the bureaucrats. He must have thought that since I was playing golf here, I naturally believed in his cause. It was like taxes were almost a physical pain for him, a sort of acute osteoarthritis that caused him constant suffering. I think he was waiting for me to let go on the big bad taxman who had made my life miserable too, a little like two people would complain together about their chronic rheumatism.

"This is it," he said.

We stopped in front of a gleaming chalet, ideally situated at the bottom of the slopes. Sitting in front of the door was a big, brand-new, four-wheel-drive BMW. *Yes, life is so hard for the poor riches!* I thought. But the worst part was that he seemed sincere. It seemed he must really suffer in the flesh when he had to write his tax check every year. Maybe rich people are convinced they deserve their money. They didn't steal it, so it's unfair to tax them, isn't it?

The Charms of Belgium

Two years ago, I ran into Nathalie (her name has been changed), an old school friend, in an airport. We hadn't seen each other in years, so we caught up on each other's news. She had two children, a girl and a boy, and was leaving in a few hours for a winter vacation in Mauritius. Michael, her husband, would be joining her in a few days. They needed some rest because, she explained, they had just moved. A Parisian family living in the beautiful Marais, they had decided to move to Brussels six months earlier.

"Huh, that's interesting," I said without thinking. "Why Brussels?"

"Michael sold his company last year. You might have seen it in the news. And with the wealth tax," she added, lowering her voice, "we just thought that Brussels would be better."

Oh yeah, of course! Brussels, with its charming accent, its fries, its dry weather, and most of all, its very soft tax rates. I realized I had put my foot in it. "I see. So do you like it there? How's the local cuisine?"

"To be honest, it's a little hard," she answered, embarrassed. She had always been rather direct; that was part of her charm.

"What do you mean?"

"We don't know anyone, and there's not much to do. But the worst is that I'm far from my family. I miss them. But it seems there is a great community. We just have to find our place." She looked at her feet while talking to me.

I continued—rather awkwardly, I have to admit. "Was it really worth earning money if it's only for being bored in a place you don't like?"

"Yeah, I know, I know," she answered. "But with a little patience, it's bound to improve. Michael says we just have to hang in there." She forced a smile, but there was sadness in her eyes.

I didn't push. I felt bad for her. Just hang in there? Really? When they had all they needed to live happily on the banks of the Seine? And this was all in the interest of optimizing their taxes. Was it really worth it?

Tax neurosis is a very common pathology among the wealthy. It sometimes has unexpected symptoms. I recall a weekend at the beach, where my wife and I had been invited to visit some friends. We had just gone to the garden to have a drink when we saw a shiny Porsche Cayenne pull up in front of the house. A couple in their thirties got out. He was wearing a handsome navy blue blazer and a signet ring. She had a pearl necklace, low heels, and a very chic style. Once introductions were made, the conversation started. I learned he was an entrepreneur in organizing events, and she worked part-time in his company.

At one point, the young woman leaned to me and asked me straightaway, "Did you happen to keep your tollbooth tickets for the trip here?"

"My tollbooth tickets?" I asked, confused. I didn't have any idea what she meant.

"Yes, it's what we always do when we go away for a weekend," she explained in the most natural way. "We collect tollbooth tickets. That way, Chris can expense them. I thought that if you kept your tickets and didn't need them, we could have them."

It took me a few seconds to realize what I had just heard. Not only did this clean-cut couple practice the misuse of company expenses like other people brush their teeth, but to glean a few extra bucks, this young woman wasn't the least bit troubled by begging a total stranger for some more slips. Taxphobia has a logic all its own.

My Friendly Financial Adviser's Bright Ideas

Tax optimization is a sport that can quickly become acrobatic. The private banking sector thrives thanks to the wealthy's obsession with reducing their taxes. Financial advisers have countless tasty stories about their rich clients. Ever since I appeared on their radar, an army of bankers in Prada suits and Gucci ties have come knocking at my door, their briefcases filled with bright ideas.

One highly motivated financial adviser who managed to pin me down for a meeting said, "Mr. Rudelle, we can offer you a wide range of services to make your money work for you."

"I have to admit that I don't have much time to think about it."

"Of course, that's what all of our entrepreneur clients say. Nevertheless, it's important to think about your assets. I can set you up with high-yield products—up to 6 percent before taxes."

"You know, with Criteo I've made one thousand times my initial investment. So …" I was a little embarrassed to cut him off so abruptly, especially since the rate of return he was offering was very attractive. But talking about financial investments really wasn't my cup of tea.

Of course, it would take a lot more than that to discourage this friendly financial adviser. He continued, "Exactly. Regarding your equity in Criteo, I suggest you place it in a holding company in Luxembourg. That would eliminate a large part of the tax friction related to your move to the United States."

Tax friction? Sometimes, the circumlocutions of bankers are pure poetry. How could I tactfully explain to this gentleman that I didn't really care about tax friction? And that the very idea of a holding company in Luxembourg was like the sound of chalk scraping a blackboard to my ears?

"Thanks, but I'm not interested," I said, politely declining. "That all seems too complicated to me, and I have to admit, I don't feel comfortable with the idea."

"Why? I can assure you that it is a perfectly legal arrangement that we have set up dozens of times. We're a serious bank, and we would never advise our clients to overstep the mark."

Overstep the mark—I wondered if that's what advisers from the big English bank recently implicated in a major fraud scandal had said. I didn't know how to explain to this financial adviser that all of these tax havens, no matter how legal they are, seem to go against the trend of history. The leniency big nations show for small countries that create artificial prosperity by tax arbitrage can't last forever. For the moment, it seems to be tolerated by the world, including this banker, who was such a stickler about the law.

My adviser realized that Luxembourg wasn't the right angle of attack. So he tried a new tactic. "I should also stress the importance of preserving your capital and making it yield a long-term profit. You have to think about your children, what you want to leave them as an inheritance. To optimize the assets transmitted, you have to plan long in advance. Our teams have lots of creative solutions in this domain."

Lots of creative solutions? That's a good one. Something to soften the idea of being six feet under. I answered, "Don't bother. I've been really lucky to get where I am today. It seems normal that my heirs will pay heavy inheritance taxes. My children have all they need to get a good start in life. And too much money won't necessarily help them."

He looked at me with silent consternation. That I wanted to pay my taxes without batting an eyelid was troubling enough to him. But that I was crazy enough to want my kids to pay a lot too was more than he could comprehend. He hesitated for a few seconds and then recovered quickly and played his last card.

"Okay, well, at least consider your situation in the States. I'd like to draw your attention to your residence status. We strongly advise expatriates not to ask for a green card because then you will be taxed on your worldwide income by the IRS, even after you leave the United States."

"Sorry, I've already applied for a green card."

"Too bad."

"Too bad?"

"In California, you're going to pay much higher taxes than in France."

It made me laugh to hear my banker bragging about France's mild taxes compared to the United States! He probably used the same language when he explained to his clients that France was a tax hell and that the only solution was to move to Belgium.

Taxes, a Practical Necessity

Some time ago, Stephen King published an article on the Internet titled "Tax Me, for F@%&'s Sake!" This prolific author of more than fifty successful novels is one of the rare contemporary writers to have become rich from book royalties. In this short, colorful text he explains why he thinks it's not normal to be taxed at only a 28 percent rate on his income (he lives in Maine): "The U.S. senators and representatives who refuse even to consider raising taxes on the rich—they squeal like scalded babies every time the subject comes up—are not, by and large, superrich themselves, although many are millionaires and all have had the equivalent of Obamacare for years. They simply idolize the rich. Don't ask me why; I don't get it either, since most rich people are as boring as old, dead dog shit."

I will leave Stephen King to answer for his delightful comments. The writer continues: "I guess some of this mad right-wing love comes from the idea that in America, anyone can become a Rich Guy if he just works hard and saves his pennies." Yes, it's true—that is still the spirit of the American dream, except today upward mobility is getting a little slim. For

Stephen King, paying one's taxes should be a patriotic act. He concludes without beating around the bush that getting the rich to pay up "has to happen if America wants to remain strong and true to its ideals. It's a practical necessity and a moral imperative."

Building any large fortune relies in part on chance. Excluding heirs, who are lucky enough to be born, a self-made businessperson who succeeds was lucky to be at the right place at the right time. This doesn't in any way play down his or her value or pugnacity. But all of that person's skills were able to matter only because the circumstances were favorable. Without a minimum of fairy godmothers, even the most talented and willing entrepreneur can't succeed. And without a society that guarantees the physical safety of people and respect of the law, it is very difficult to build a solid business.

Of course, success is fragile too. It's only one step from the summit to the abyss. But in periods without war or major catastrophes, once an estate is built and liquid, it is relatively easy to preserve. In their safe and comfortable existence, the wealthy sometimes forget what they owe to the rest of society, what allows them to enjoy their good fortune with peace of mind. Taxes are not always just an unjust robbery.

Silicon Valley, Its Millionaires, and Its Poor

Silicon Valley offers a particularly interesting overview of tomorrow's world. This is where many products that are shaping the future are conceived. It's also where you can witness certain social imbalances linked to this technology revolution. We certainly haven't reached the stage described in Aldous Huxley's *Brave New World*, but it is hard to deny that the winners of the system are taking more and more of the cake. This dream machine draws talented people from around the world, who come to get their tickets to the great tech lottery. Breathtaking wealth is concentrated among a handful of winners, which naturally encourages a constant stream of newcomers to try their luck.

There was a twenty-five-year-old immigrant who started with nothing and became a billionaire in just a few years. I'm thinking of the extraordinary story of Jan Koum. The son of a cleaning lady and a foreman, he spent his childhood in the Ukraine in a house without running water. When he was sixteen, his family immigrated to the United States. The teen worked part-time cleaning a corner grocery store and waited in line for food stamps in front of stores in Mountain View. He managed to get a job and Yahoo! but quickly got bored. Then he created a little application for mobile phones, WhatsApp. This instant messaging system succeeded when at the same time many others fell flat on their face. Five years later, Facebook acquired his company for $19 billion. It's hard to find a more perfect example of the American dream.

Wealth creation has never been as high in the Valley, which is supposedly home to fifty billionaires and ten thousand millionaires. The town of Atherton, which is adjacent to Palo Alto, has the highest housing values in the United States. It's impossible to find a house for less than $3 million, and homes are often twice that price. In the hills overlooking the valley, the new moguls build extravagant ranches. Nevertheless, they remain a tiny minority compared to the population of California. At the time it was purchased, WhatsApp had only fifty employees. They really hit the jackpot. But at the same time, what better illustration of this winner-takes-all trend?

Behind all these well-known fairy tales, this world also has its dark side, the thousands of unlucky nobodies whose start-ups never took off. And most of all, despite this abundance of wealth, there are more and more homeless people in San Francisco and the Valley living in their cars or makeshift camps, sometimes just a couple hundred yards from shiny mansions. The tech revolution is fascinating, but not everyone benefits from it. A significant part of the population is left by the wayside.

The Rise of Inequality

In his best seller *Capital in the Twenty-First Century*, economist Thomas Piketty analyzes the historical dimension of this phenomenon of wealth concentration. The central idea of his book is that since average return on equity is structurally higher than overall economic growth, rich people tend to become richer over time. The only things that can counter this concentration of wealth are progressive tax rates or major shocks such as world wars or depressions (which no one wants, of course).

For weeks, this rather dry and heavy tome, moreover written by an obscure French economist, unexpectedly found itself on the top of the best-seller list in the United States. Piketty's thesis found such an audience in America notably because of the explosion of inequalities in the past thirty years in the world's largest economy. The Reagan tax revolution saw the marginal tax rate drop sharply compared to the previous decades. While large fortunes skyrocketed, modest incomes stagnated. Two-thirds of American growth was swept up by 1 percent of the population. The extent of inequalities is even more stunning if we focus on the richest 0.1 percent or even the richest 0.01 percent. By hitting where it hurts, this book teases the foundation of the American dream. With upward mobility limited to the lucky few, this new evolution hits at the heart of the American identity, which, it is worth remembering, was built in the eighteenth century on the myth of equal opportunities in reaction to the Old World, where a tiny slice of the aristocracy had all the privileges.

My wife and I have a running joke when we are invited to someone's house for dinner. I ask her, "What do you say to some Piketty time tonight?" That's our code for dropping the bomb of conversation about inequalities during dessert. There's nothing like it to suddenly raise the tension around the table.

Generally, people react quickly. A classic response is basic denial: "But who can prove that inequalities are increasing? More falsehoods from journalists. There are plenty of statistics that prove the opposite." (Don't ask them for their sources, though; this really irks them.)

Then there are the social Darwinists. At least they have the merit of taking a clear and coherent position: "Inequalities aren't bad. On the contrary, inequalities allow society to become more efficient. This is called meritocracy, and it's our strength."

If I wanted to be a little cynical, I could translate that to "Who cares about inequalities as long as I'm on the winning side?" The argument still deserves a little attention. If you are comfortable with the idea of a segregated world, with a minority of super rich on one side, hiding themselves in gated communities protected like Fort Knox, and the rest of the world not seeing much progress, what's wrong with that? Economic growth is supposed to solve the problem of inequalities. The rich invest, creating jobs, which makes the economy thrive, and everyone wins in the end. After all, why be offended that the rich get richer if the poor also become a little less poor? This seems like implacable logic—except that, as we have seen, the statistics in the United States over the past thirty years invalidate this nice thesis. The fact that economic growth has benefited only a very small minority is quite disturbing. Furthermore, there is a lot of speculation around work being replaced by more and more intelligent machines (yes, it's coming). This will further empower the winners and can only accelerate this trend toward wealth concentration.

What about the social ladder? The American dream founded on self-made men who started with nothing? The first problem is that inequalities have the nasty tendency to continue through generations. Children from underprivileged backgrounds statistically have much less chance of succeeding than the well-off—and this despite all of the public policy efforts to reduce this gap. Most of all, with the digital revolution, the social ladder has become a miniscule supersonic elevator. For the winners who are lucky to have joined a successful start-up, the rise to the top is very fast. But nationwide, this affects only a very small percentage of people.

Do you think I'm being too pessimistic? Whether we like it or not, I have the feeling we are heading toward a world in which the rich will have to get used to paying more taxes. It's the logical consequence of this winner-takes-all digital revolution. And when I refer to rich people who should be taxed more, I include myself. This provocative idea is triggering a general outcry. Still, I was very surprised when I arrived in Palo Alto to witness election campaigns led by candidates who bragged about raising local taxes to offer more public services. Seen through the European lens, this fiscal one-upmanship seemed surrealistic.

Reading Piketty, I've also discovered that super high tax brackets existed in the United States fifty years ago. As he mentions in his book, "between 1930 and 1980, the upper level tax rate on incomes over $1 million was 82% on average. Not only did this not kill American capitalism, but there was more growth in the United States from 1950 to 1970 than there has been since the 1980s." Correlation doesn't mean causality. Imposing a marginal rate of 80 percent today would not give us the economic growth rates of the postwar years. Nevertheless, it is sometimes worth remembering that some tax rates that seem aberrant in today's context were well accepted for decades in the very country that incarnated the free-market system.

Epilogue

July 2016

My dad died last December, so I guess my siblings and I are next in line—hopefully not too soon, though. All parents know the feeling of pride in seeing their children grow up. In family albums, we are filled with wonder as we record the first steps, the first teeth, the first book read, the first diploma received (in the United States, this starts at the end of primary school with a ceremony worthy of a PhD). This pride always comes with a twinge of sorrow, a wave of nostalgia for the past. My daughters are now teenagers. They spontaneously mix French with American English, in sentences that resemble gobbledygook, forcing me to kindly ask them to repeat. Like all adolescents, they have their own world, their own music that I don't listen to, their own codes of behavior that I don't understand. One day, they will leave the house; they won't need me or their mother anymore and will fly with their own wings.

Entrepreneurs experience something similar with their start-ups. In the beginning, you don't sleep, like stressed-out, young parents who remain keenly attuned to their baby's breathing. You are afraid of going off-track too soon, of the fundraising that may not come. And then come all the "first times"—the first meeting with investors, the first closing, the first big client, and finally, the IPO, of course. It's a little like your child graduating from high school, both the end of a cycle and the beginning of the next one. Since Criteo went public, a new life has started. Little by little, the company has acquired its own dynamic, all while continuing to grow. After the IPO, Franck decided to leave, with the desire to launch a new start-up and feel the excitement of beginning again, with everything still to be written. Romain, however, became more involved than ever in the Criteo adventure. After having led the rise of our technical team, he gave himself the challenge of managing human resources for the whole company.

I have had the extraordinary chance to lead this adventure for all these years. At each new stage of growth, I had to reinvent my own role. Leading a start-up of ten, fifty, three hundred, or two thousand people is never the same experience. The stakes and challenges are completely different at every level, as are the methods that work. You have to constantly kill the winning recipes from previous stages and reinvent new ways of working. To keep growing, you want to hire the best possible professionals in each position. And you want to delegate ever more significant parts of operations. I believe that if you continue to try to manage everything yourself, you eventually become your own bottleneck.

Over the years, I brought in many very talented experts. That started with technology with Franck and Romain. Then came sales, operations, and finance. My role has gradually evolved from the *how* to the *why*. Why are we going in this direction when another would be an impasse? Why does this product match Criteo's DNA, whereas another product would risk leading us astray? I see myself as a scout who explores and articulates our long-term vision.

As parents allow their children to fly with their own wings, the time has come to hand over the day-to-day reins. As a matter of fact, I transitioned in December 2015 to executive chairman. At the same time, we announced the promotion of Eric Eichmann as our new CEO. This evolution was planned well in advance. When I hired Eric three years earlier, I had this idea in the back of my mind. Quickly, Eric showed solid achievements in the missions he was put in charge of. From sales and operations, his role expanded into marketing, R&D, product, HR, and finance. Eric is now in charge of driving the Criteo wonderful machine toward our next phase of growth.

The big idea of Criteo has always been to focus on actionable consumer intent. Capturing and targeting more of this intent will allow us to further expand our addressable market. For the billions they invest in marketing, advertisers want to see actual sales and revenues. This obsession with measurable performances has been a key success factor for Criteo. And our clients love it. Their trust in us makes me so proud.

I reread these pages, and I see how far we have come. I never imagined we would reach such a scale. I have the incredible luck to wake up each morning and ask myself what the day has in store for me. My agenda fills up extremely fast, and I fight to give myself enough bandwidth to achieve my goals. My professional life of incessant travel eats up a significant piece of my family time. My friends sometimes ask me, "Why do you continue?" And I too sometimes wonder what makes me jump out of bed every day, race through my e-mail, hop on a plane, and simply go on with this. After all, I could drop everything and go on some permanent vacation.

I already mentioned in the first pages that I always wanted to create my own company. But as I reach the end of this book, I want to make a confession to the reader. When I started my career at twenty-four, I was utterly convinced that I would immediately stop working as soon as I had achieved reasonable financial success. Where did I get this idea? During my high school years, I worked myself numb, cramming for science classes without experiencing that much pleasure. When I was finally admitted to a good college, I transformed overnight into a first-rate idler. I skipped nearly all my lectures and did the strict minimum to remain afloat, to the extent that in my final year I nearly didn't receive my diploma. I still remember the very harsh sermon the dean gave me, telling me I was a disgrace to the institution. As a result, it was clear to me that I was deeply and truly lazy, just capable of making an effort when the stakes were really high.

During my first years in the professional world, I was bored to death, which reinforced this conviction. Professional life seemed to be anything but fulfilling, and I was determined to get out of it as fast as I could, by any means necessary. Starting my own business and earning enough money to never have to go to the office again seemed like the shortest way to this precious freedom. Of course, I didn't envision sitting on the sofa all day watching television and drinking beer (plus, I don't like beer anyway). But I pictured a wonderful life of traveling and reading, seasoned with parties and philosophical discussions until early morning, a bit like aristocrats during the Enlightenment, who lived idle, carefree lives.

The question came up first after I sold Kiwee. I had earned enough money to retire and travel around the world, all while keeping a nest egg for when I wanted to return to a sedentary lifestyle, on the condition that I had to live modestly, which suited me very well. But in the meantime, I had started a family, with two daughters who were just of school age.

I quickly realized that a life of eternal travels wasn't ideal for kids, who demand stability to develop their personalities. In a way, I didn't want to deprive my daughters of a normal childhood with their own social lives. So we opted for a sedentary life. One thing led to another, and soon I felt the desire to launch another start-up.

Today, I have earned more than enough money for a very comfortable life, and I hear this recurring question again: "So when are you going to stop?" It has become a refrain when I go back to France. For my compatriots, this is their polite way of asking about my well-being. I guess that despite the revolution, there must be an old fascination with idle aristocrats in Europe. On the other hand, I notice that no one asks me this question in the United States. Here, it would seem almost incongruous.

So I'm this truly lazy guy who keeps justifying why he keeps working. So why do I?

The first thing that comes to my mind is intellectual curiosity. Building a start-up is one of the most stimulating experiences I could possibly imagine. When you face highly varied situations, new challenges incessantly appear, and sometimes the most established beliefs must be completely revisited. I feel like I learn something new every day. What could be better for a person who hates routine?

There is probably also another, deeper force driving me. Each time I've launched a new project, I've had to convince talents to quit comfortable jobs to join me, convince investors to put money into the venture, and eventually convince clients to work with us. Overall, it took many people to trust me. To deserve this trust, I almost feel I have to "do my duty," even though I am aware that this outdated phrase sounds silly. This strange sense of duty puzzles me. I suspect this trait took root in the rigid ethics my mother hammered during my childhood. My mother drew her unique personal philosophy from a mix of Protestant intellectualism and a subtle Jewish tradition that had been buried in the previous generation. This uncompromising, ascetic spirit was very far removed from the casual Catholicism that ruled in my father's family. As a young man, I thought I was more from the hedonistic paternal side, and my mother's lectures annoyed me. In hindsight, I realize that I am much closer to her than I had wanted to admit.

At forty-seven, I have won the freedom I was always seeking, even if it doesn't look how I had pictured it. I've benefited a lot from the start-up ecosystem, and I aspire to also contribute myself. For a long time, that just meant growing Criteo as big as possible. Today, Criteo has become a source of inspiration for many entrepreneurs. So now I'm also looking at new ways to participate in the grand tech adventure.

With this perspective, I have financed the Galion Project, a non-profit think tank for start-up founders. The idea is to help ambitious entrepreneurs scale their start-ups more smoothly and quickly through best-practice sharing. Leveraging veterans in the field, we do this typically through three-day trips, in nice locations where we mix kite surfing and working sessions. Collectively, we try to identify what best practices can be shared across the start-up ecosystem. These sessions also result in research papers and actionable tools.

For instance, our first project was to build a standard term-sheet document for series A. We realized that there is a structural asymmetry between first-time entrepreneurs who negotiate with investors for the first time in their lives and VCs who've done dozens of deals. Entrepreneurs fear being abused. This asymmetry creates suspicions and friction in the discussions. To address the issue, we gathered fifty seasoned entrepreneurs in San Francisco, New York, and Paris to brainstorm and come up with deal terms that would guarantee a fair balance between the two parties. Because those terms can potentially have so much impact on a founder's life, there have been a lot of passionate discussions on the topic. The spirit was not to come up with a document outrageously in favor of entrepreneurs; that would have been worthless. What we were aiming to do was find win-win solutions with financial investors on difficult topics such as rights of first refusal and founder's leaver clause.

The Galion Term Sheet was a big hit. In the first twenty-four hours after we put it online, it was downloaded more than 1,500 times. Furthermore, a dozen tier-one VCs immediately supported the initiative, which built its credibility even more. This open-source document is not set in stone and is meant to be a starting point for negotiations. But I already have several testimonies from entrepreneurs, investors, and lawyers that the Galion Term Sheet template has facilitated actual rounds of financing. Nothing could make me happier. As I write these lines, the Galion Project is working on a number of other critical start-up-specific best practices such as board governance, scaling overseas, and top talent acquisition.

Now that I'm more visible in the tech rain forest, I'm also getting a lot of e-mails from young entrepreneurs seeking funds for their start-ups. Rather than just playing the lonely business angel, I've decided to coinvest with Franck and Romain. We believe we bring to the table an expertise different from and complementary to the big VCs, especially in areas such as machine learning and international expansion. If the experience we've accumulated through Criteo could be useful to others, it would give me tremendous satisfaction.

Obviously, I'm also brainstorming on the next BIG thing. But it's way too early to discuss this here... No matter what, the future belongs to the geeks. It's going to be so much fun. As we like to say at Criteo: go, Go, GO!

About the Author

JB Rudelle founded Criteo in 2005 and drove its growth into a global organization. In January 2016, he transitioned from CEO to Chairman, where his focus is on the long-term strategic vision of the company.